# 观察

王骥 马静 编译

**Observation**

**世事** 纷扰
每个人都是 **观察者**、评论员
新鲜的视角、经典的论述
以及具有启迪性的思辨
无不充实我们的智慧背囊

**高端导读版**
**[时事卷]**

天津教育出版社

**图书在版编目(CIP)数据**

观察／王骥,马静编译. —天津:天津教育出版社,2012.1
(美丽英文;高端导读版)
ISBN 978-7-5309-6638-9
Ⅰ.①观… Ⅱ.①王… ②马… Ⅲ.①英语—汉语—对照读物
②随笔—作品集—世界 Ⅳ.①H319.4:I

中国版本图书馆 CIP 数据核字(2011)第 268254 号

---

**美丽英文·高端导读版 观察**

| | |
|---|---|
| 出 版 人 | 胡振泰 |
| 编 译 | 王 骥 马 静 |
| 选题策划 | 袁 颖 王艳超 |
| 责任编辑 | 田 昕 |
| 装帧设计 | 郭亚非 |
| 出版发行 | 天津教育出版社 |
| | 天津市和平区西康路 35 号 邮政编码 300051 |
| | http://www.tjeph.com.cn |
| 经 销 | 新华书店 |
| 印 刷 | 天津新华二印刷有限公司 |
| 版 次 | 2012 年 1 月第 1 版 |
| 印 次 | 2012 年 1 月第 1 次印刷 |
| 规 格 | 16 开(787mm×1092mm) |
| 字 数 | 120 千字 |
| 印 张 | 12.75 |
| 定 价 | 24.00 元 |

观察 OBSERVATION

# Content

A Successful China Can Make U.S. More Prosperous / 001
中国成功会促进美国繁荣

Paris Conference Contemplates Libya's Future / 007
巴黎会议思索利比亚未来

An Anti-nuclear Protest in Japan / 013
日本上演反核游行

Wall Street Protests Continue And Grow Across the Country / 020
华尔街抗议活动仍在继续,并向全美蔓延

California Bans Shark Fin / 027
美国加州颁布"鱼翅"禁令

Three Americans Share 2011 Nobel Prize in Physics / 034
三位美国科学家分享2011年诺贝尔物理学奖

Putin Urges Choice on Admitting Russia to World Trade Organization / 041
普京敦促尽快做出决定接纳俄罗斯加入世贸组织

Higher Production Costs Shift Chinese Manufacturing / 048
成本升高迫使中国厂商撤离沿海省份

Afghanistan 10 Years Later / 055
10年战后阿富汗

U.S. And North Korea Meet on Nuclear Issue / 062
美朝核会谈

Drug War in Mexico Raises Human Rights Concerns / 068
墨西哥打击贩毒引发人权担忧

Thousands Gather to Dedicate Martin Luther King Jr. Memorial / 074
万人集会为马丁·路德·金纪念园揭幕

Europe Rushes to Contain Debt Crisis / 081
欧洲加紧遏制债务危机

20 Years On: Economic Reform in India / 088
印度经济改革20年

Study Shows Diabetes Surging Worldwide / 095
研究表明糖尿病正冲击全球

Reaping the Rewards of Risk-Taking / 101
播下风险种，收获大苹果

Ukraine's Joan of Arc, Whose Conviction Caused Europeans' Dissatisfaction / 108
乌克兰"圣女贞德"获刑引起欧洲不满

How to Lose Friends And Alienate People? / 115
默多克众叛亲离？

Barack Obama: Can Anybody Beat Him? / 122
美国总统大选，奥巴马无人能敌？

Amazon: The Walmart of the Web / 129
亚马逊：网上沃尔玛

Famine in Somalia: A Man-made Crisis / 136
人造危机：索马里饥荒

Race to the Moon for Private Firms / 142
私有公司登月竞赛

Money Really Can't Buy Love / 149
金钱买不了真爱

观 察 OBSERVATION

London Olympics, Tourism or Not? / 154
伦敦奥运会堪比旅游经济?

The Secret to Berlusconi's Dolce Vita / 161
贝卢斯科尼立足政坛的五种武器

Nation's Mood at Lowest Level in Two Years, Poll Shows / 169
美国人民不高兴

The 10 Memorial Service of 911 / 176
"9·11事件"10周年纪念

The Rise of the Redback / 183
美元,一家独大何时休

Universities Should Work Together, Not Compete / 188
大学需要合作,而非竞争

Veterans Day for No More War / 193
为和平而生的"老兵节"

观 察 OBSERVATION

**Reading Guidance**

2011年8月17日至22日期间,美国副总统拜登访华。此时,正值美国主权债务评级下调、美国大选前夕的关键时刻,作为美国政坛上的重量级人物,拜登此次中国之行备受关注。《华尔街日报》《纽约时报》等媒体认为,拜登访华是为了表明:美国将确保中国所持有的美债安全。21日,拜登在四川大学的演讲中谈到,美债危机主要是由于美国民主党、共和党的分歧造成的,美债还是安全的。他希望中国人放心,美国会把经济搞上去。除此之外,双方就广泛的双边、地区和全球问题进行了磋商。

本文由美国副总统约瑟夫·R.拜登(Joseph R. Biden Jr.)撰写,发表在2011年9月9日的《纽约时报》(*New York Times*)上。

# A Successful China Can Make U. S. More Prosperous

I first visited China in 1979, a few months after our countries normalized relations. China was just beginning to remake its economy, and I was in the first Senate delegation to witness this evolution. Traveling through the country last month, I could see how much China had changed in 32 years—and yet the

debate about its remarkable rise remains familiar.

Then, as now, there were concerns about what a growing China meant to America and the world. Some here and in the region see China's growth as a threat, entertaining visions of a cold-war-style rivalry or great-power confrontation. Some Chinese worry that our aim in the Asia-Pacific is to contain China's rise.

I reject these views. I remain convinced that a successful China can make our country more prosperous, not less.

As trade and investment bind us together, we have a stake in each other's success. On issues from global security to global economic growth, we share common challenges and responsibilities—and we have incentives to work together. That is why our administration has worked to put our relationship on a stable footing.

We often focus on Chinese exports to America, but last year American companies exported more than $100 billion worth of goods and services to China, supporting hundreds of thousands of jobs here. In fact, our exports to China have been growing much faster than our exports to the rest of the world.

The Chinese leaders I met with know their country must shift from an economy driven by exports, investment and heavy industry to one driven more by consumption and services. This includes continued steps to revalue their currency and to provide fair access to their markets. As Americans save more and Chinese buy more, this transition will accelerate, opening opportunities for us.

Even as the United States and China cooperate, we also compete. I strongly believe that the United States can and will flourish from this competition.

First, we need to keep China's rising economic power in perspective. According to the International Monetary Fund, America's gross domestic product, almost $15 trillion, is still more than twice as large as China's; our per-capita G.D.P., above $47000, is 11 times China's.

And while there is a lot of talk about China's "owning" America's debt, the truth is that Americans own America's debt. China holds just 8 percent of outstanding Treasury securities. By comparison, Americans hold nearly 70 percent. Our unshakable commitment to honoring our financial obligations is for the sake of Americans, as well as for those overseas. It is why the United States has never defaulted on its obligations and never will.

Maybe more important, the nature of 21st-century competition favors the United States. In the 20th century, we measured a nation's wealth primarily by its natural resources, its land mass, its population and its army. In the 21st century, the true wealth of a nation is found in the creative minds of its people and their ability to innovate.

As I told students in Chengdu, the United States is hard-wired for innovation. Competition is in the very fabric of our society. It has enabled each generation of Americans to give life to world-changing ideas—from the cotton gin to the airplane, the microchip, the Internet.

We owe our strength to our political and economic system and to the way we educate our children—not merely to accept established orthodoxy but to challenge and improve it. We not only tolerate but celebrate free expression and vigorous debate. The rule of law protects private property, lends predictability to investments, and ensures accountability for poor and wealthy alike. Our universities remain the ultimate destination for the world's students and scholars. And we welcome immigrants with skill, ambition and the desire to better their lives.

We need to ensure that any American willing to work can find a good job. We need to keep attracting the world's top talent. We must continue to invest in the fundamental sources of our strength: education, infrastructure and innovation. But our future is in our own hands. If we take bold steps, there is no reason America won't emerge stronger than ever.

As vice president, I've traveled half a million miles around the world. I always come home feeling the same confidence in our future. Some may warn of

America's demise, but I'm not among them. And let me reassure you: based on my time in China, neither are the Chinese.

**Notes**

incentive：刺激，鼓励
per-capita：人均
default：不履行义务；违约；弃权
hard-wired：根深蒂固的
orthodoxy：正统观念
infrastructure：结构，基础设施
demise：衰亡

# 中国成功会促进美国繁荣

我首次访问中国是在1979年两国关系正常化几个月后。当时，中国刚刚开始重建经济，我作为第一个参议院访华代表团的成员见证了这个演变的阶段。上个月再次访问中国，我发现中国在32年中发生的变化十分巨大，令人瞩目，然而由此引发的争论依然似曾相识。

那时，如同现在一样，有人担心日益强大的中国对美国和全世界意味着什么。在美国和亚太地区的某些人视中国的崛起为一种威胁，津津乐道地谈论冷战式的对峙或大国间的对抗。有些中国人担心，我们在亚太地区的目标是遏制中国的崛起。

对于这样的观点我无法苟同。我坚信，中国的成功会促进我国的繁

## 观察 OBSERVATION

荣,并不会起反作用。

两国的贸易和投资往来密切,所以各自的成功又相互依存。从全球安全到全球经济增长等诸多问题,美中两国都面临共同的挑战,肩负共同的责任。因此,两国有合作的动力。这就是我国政府致力于保持两国关系稳定的原因。

我们一直十分关注中国对美国的出口,但去年美国公司向中国出口了价值1000多亿美元的产品和服务,给美国提供了数十万个就业岗位。事实上,美国对中国出口的增长速度远远超过我们对世界其他地区的出口。

我会见过的中国领导人都明白,中国必须从出口、投资和重工业推动的经济转向更多地由消费与服务推动的经济。这包括继续重估人民币的币值和保证市场的公平准入。随着美国人增加储蓄,中国人扩大消费,这一转型将加速进行,从而为我们创造机会。

美中两国在合作的同时,也在相互竞争。我坚信,美国可以而且必将通过这场竞争兴旺发达。

首先,我们需要恰当地看待中国经济力量的增长。据国际货币基金组织提供的数据,美国的国内生产总值接近15万亿美元,仍为中国国内生产总值的两倍多;我国的人均国内生产总值是47000多美元,是中国人均国内生产总值的11倍。

人们常常对中国"持有"美国债权一事议论纷纷,但实际情况是,是美国人本身持有美国的债权。中国仅持有8%未偿还的财政部债券,而美国人持有将近70%。我们承诺毫不动摇地履行我们的金融责任,不仅为了海外持有人的利益,也是为了美国人民的利益。这就是美国从未发生债务违约且永远不会违约的原因。

也许更重要的是,21世纪的竞争在本质上有利于美国。20世纪,我们主要通过自然资源、陆地面积、人口和军队衡量一个国家的财富。21世纪,一个国家真正的财富在于人民的创造性思维和创新能力。

就像我在成都对中国学生讲的那样,美国在创新方面得天独厚。竞争是我国社会结构的有机组成部分。竞争使世世代代的美国人将改变世界的构想变为现实——从轧棉机到飞机、微型芯片、国际互联网等等。

我们把我们的实力归功于我们的政治和经济制度，归功于我们教育子女的方式——对已经确立的正统观念，不单是接受，而是敢于挑战和加以改进。我们不仅接纳，而且鼓励自由表达和激烈的辩论。法制保护私人财产，提供投资的可预见性，责有攸归，无论贫富。我们的大学仍然是全世界学生和学者最向往的目的地。我们欢迎有技能、有雄心和渴望改善自己生活的移民。

我们必须保证任何愿意工作的美国人都能找到一份好工作。我们需要继续吸引全世界的顶尖人才。我们必须继续为我国实力的根基进行投资：教育、基础设施和创新。但我们的未来掌握在我们自己手中。如果我们采取大胆的措施，美国没有任何理由不比以往更繁荣昌盛。

我作为副总统访问世界各地，已经走过50万英里。每次回国，我都对我们的未来抱着同样的信心。有些人可能要提醒美国的衰落，但我不这样认为。我想让你们放心：根据我在中国的了解，中国人也不这样认为。

## More to Read

拜登在美债危机达到最高潮时访华，外界将这次访问冠以"抚慰之旅"的名称是比较恰当的。拜登在中国的访问除了与中国领导层举行会谈交换意见之外，其亮点反而在于"公众外交"方面，从在鼓楼的姚记炒肝店吃一顿79元的廉价午餐，再到四川访问过程中参观地震灾区新建的学校、观看学生的篮球比赛，他更希望通过自己的民间交往拉近与中国普通民众的关系。作为美国的副总统，他的一言一行所代表的都是美国的国家利益，因此他在中国的亲善举动同其在美国国内的强硬表态并不矛盾。都是为了最大限度地维护美国的超强地位，对外塑造美国亲善友好之国际形象，对内提振士气、凝聚共识。中国当前已然被美国当做头号竞争者，这种软硬兼施的策略值得我们警醒和思考。

观察 OBSERVATION

**Reading Guidance**

1969年9月1日,卡扎菲率领一批军官发动政变,执掌大权。颇具讽刺意味的是,整整42年后的2011年9月1日,一场讨论利比亚"后卡扎菲时代"战后政治、经济重建的"利比亚之友"国际会议在法国首都巴黎开幕。此时,绝大多数的欧美国家已经正式承认利比亚全国过渡委员会为利比亚的合法政权。这一刻距离利比亚内战爆发只不过半年时间而已。短短6个月,在利比亚经营了40余年的卡扎菲政权就灰飞烟灭了。在这场战争中为反对派"贡献良多"的西方国家已经开始着手制定利比亚战后重建蓝图。巨大的石油利益如何分配也是这些国家最为关切的问题之一。

# Paris Conference Contemplates Libya's Future

World leaders are gathering in France Thursday to discuss Libya's future after Moammar Gadhafi and Russia became the latest country to recognize the National Transitional Council (NTC) as the country's legitimate authority. The conference in Paris brings together officials from 60 countries, including those that have backed the NTC for months as well as those that have not recognized

the temporary authority. Officials expect NTC leader Mustafa Abdel Jalil to outline an 18-month roadmap to creating a new constitution and holding elections.

Thursday marked 42 years since Moammar Gadhafi took power in Libya. But with the longtime ruler now on the run—in an audio message aired Thursday he promised no surrender—world backers of the uprising against him met to plan rebuilding the country along new lines.

The meeting on Libya is hosted by British Prime Minister David Cameron and French President Nicolas Sarkozy. They were joined by dignitaries from around the world, including US Secretary of State Hillary Clinton and UN Secretary-General Ban Ki-moon. China and Russia are also sending representatives to the talks.

Speaking in Paris before the conference, Britain's Foreign Secretary William Hague said it shows that the world is coming together to support Libya's future.

"The other thing of course that it provides today—that the conference provides—is an opportunity for the National Transitional Council to set out their plans for the stabilization of Libya and then what they do politically to create a democratic and inclusive Libya." noted Hague.

The "Friends of Libya" conference gives the National Transitional Council (NTC) an international platform.

French Foreign Minister Alain Juppe told reporters that it is important to have confidence in the NTC leadership.

We didn't intervene in Libya, he says, for it to fall into another regime that wouldn't respect the fundamental rights of the Libyan people.

The NTC is set to push for access to billions of dollars in foreign-held Libyan assets, which were frozen while Mr. Gadhafi held power. The United States, Britain, and France have already been granted permission by the UN sanctions committee to unfreeze billions of dollars.

The NTC was also set to lay out plans for a new constitution and elections.

观察 OBSERVATION

Nicola Pratt, an expert on the international politics of the Middle East at Warwick University in Britain, says the platform that Thursday's conference provides for the NTC is important.

"The council needs financial support desperately in order to start providing basic services, to pay civil servants, to start generally rebuilding the economy," noted Pratt. "So this is a crucial period. If the NTC doesn't manage to do these things quickly, then it definitely will suffer from a lack of legitimacy."

But she says the importance of the conference is largely symbolic.

She says much of the controversy will take place in the corridors as countries compete for post-war contracts over infrastructure, utilities, and oil.

"There is going to be some competition between those countries that have played a role in helping to get rid of Gadhafi, feeling some sort of entitlement now that Gadhafi is gone and this reconstruction process is going to begin." added Pratt.

On Thursday, just ahead of the conference, Russia recognized the National Transitional Council as Libya's acting leadership. But a number of countries around the world, including some in the African Union, have not recognized the NTC as Libya's legitimate government.

U. S. President Barack Obama has called on Libyan leader Moammar Gadhafi to "relinquish power once and for all," saying the force against him has reached a turning point. In a statement after Libyan rebels pushed into the capital, Tripoli, Mr. Obama said Mr. Gadhafi needs to acknowledge that he no longer controls the country. Mr. Obama also said the United States will continue to work with the international community to support a peaceful transition to democracy in Libya, and urged the opposition Transitional National Council to include the interests of all the Libyan people.

The European Union, Britain and Italy have all said Mr. Gadhafi's rule is coming to an end, and urged the Libyan leader to step down in order to avoid more bloodshed. Meanwhile, China said Monday it "respects the choice of the

Libyan people" and hopes stability returns to the country quickly. South Africa said it is not supporting the rebels and denied reports that it had sent a plane to Libya to help Mr. Gadhafi. South Africa's Foreign Minister said Mr. Gadhafi has not and would not ask for safety in South Africa. (754words)

## Notes

uprising：起义，暴动
dignitary：显要人物
inclusive：包容的
legitimacy：合法性，正当性
symbolic：象征意义的
relinquish：放弃

# 巴黎会议思索利比亚未来

  世界各国领导人星期四在法国讨论卡扎菲之后的利比亚的未来。俄罗斯成为最新承认全国过渡委员会为利比亚合法政府的国家。在巴黎举行的这次会议云集了60个国家的官员，其中包括几个月来支持利比亚全国过渡委员会的国家和还没有承认这个临时当局的国家。有关官员希望全国过渡委员会领导人贾利勒拟出一个在18个月内制定新宪法和举行选举的路线图。

  周四是利比亚领袖卡扎菲夺取政权42周年的日子。但是这位长期的统治者现在正在逃亡——尽管他在周四的广播信息中发誓不会投降——

利比亚起义的国际支持者召开会议，商讨按照新的方针重建利比亚的计划。

这次的利比亚会议由英国首相戴维·卡梅伦和法国总统尼古拉·萨科齐主持。此外还有来自世界各地的重要人物参加，包括美国国务卿希拉里·克林顿和联合国秘书长潘基文。中国和俄罗斯也派代表参加了这次会谈。

会议开始之前，英国外交大臣威廉·黑格在巴黎发表讲话。他表示，全世界将团结起来支持利比亚的未来。

黑格提到，"这次会议的另外一个作用是，为全国过渡委员会提供一个机会，让他们制定出稳定利比亚的计划，继而让他们从政治上创建一个民主的和包容的利比亚。"

"利比亚之友"会议为全国过渡委员会提供了一个国际化平台。

法国外交部长阿兰·朱佩表示，大家必须对全国过渡委员会的领导有信心，这是非常重要的。

朱佩说，我们没有干涉利比亚，使之过渡到另一个不尊重利比亚人民基本权利的政权。

利比亚全国过渡委员会力求得到卡扎菲执政期间被冻结的存在国外的利比亚资产。美国，英国和法国已经获得联合国制裁委员会解冻数十亿美元资产的许可。

全国过渡委员会还将制定出台新宪法，并计划进行选举。

英国华威大学中东地区国际政治专家尼古拉·蒲拉特表示，周四的会议为全国过渡委员会提供的平台是非常重要的。

"为了开始提供基本的服务，为公务员支付薪资，开始重建经济，全国过渡委员会亟须经济支持。"蒲拉特说，"所以这是非常关键的时期。如果全国过渡委员会不能尽快做到这些，毫无疑问他们将缺乏合法性。"

但是她说，这次会议的重要性主要在于其象征意义。

她说，为了争夺利比亚战后基础设施，公用设施和石油方面的合同，各国之间少不了会后走廊上的争论。

"由于现在卡扎菲正在逃亡，重建工程即将开始，曾经在推翻卡扎菲的

过程中发挥过作用的国家认为自己有权获得这些合同,这些国家之间将会出现一定的竞争。"蒲拉特进一步说道。

周四的会议开始之前,俄罗斯认可全国过渡委员会为利比亚代理领导机构。但是全世界仍有很多国家没有承认全国过渡委员会为利比亚合法政府,包括非洲联盟几个国家。

美国总统奥巴马呼吁利比亚领导人卡扎菲"彻底放弃政权",并说反抗他的势头已经达到一个转折点。在利比亚反政府武装进入首都的黎波里后,奥巴马发表声明说,卡扎菲必须承认,他已经不再控制这个国家了。奥巴马还说,美国将继续与国际社会合作,支持利比亚向民主和平过渡。他还敦促反对派的全国过渡委员会考虑到所有利比亚人民的利益。

欧盟、英国和意大利都表示,利比亚领导人卡扎菲的统治正走向尽头,为避免更多的流血牺牲,卡扎菲应该下台。与此同时,中国在星期一表示"尊重利比亚人民的选择",希望利比亚局势尽快恢复稳定。南非在星期一表示不支持利比亚反对派武装,并驳斥了有关南非派遣飞机帮助卡扎菲的报导。南非外长说,卡扎菲尚未寻求、也不会要求在南非得到庇护。

**More to Read**

卡扎菲当年领导革命时也曾意气风发,指点江山。在冷战的两极格局中,他宣称既不亲苏也不靠美,走出了被称为"民众国"的"第三条道路"。然而,就是这样一个利比亚的铁腕领袖,在苦心经营了42年之后,居然一夕之间就沦落为被四处追击的逃犯,其中滋味,恐怕只有卡扎菲本人才能体会了。如果抛开北约等西方军事集团在利比亚内战中起到的作用不谈,我们仍然可以发现国内问题是卡扎菲丢失政权的重要原因。政治上的独裁统治、经济上的贫富差距导致利比亚社会的不满情绪急剧升温。因此,前一天还在称颂卡扎菲伟大的的黎波里人,在全国过渡委员会武装进入之后立即对其大加挞伐的行为也就不难理解了。

## Reading Guidance

  2011年9月11日是东京日本大地震半年纪念日。日本各地灾民举行追悼仪式，东京等各大城市则有民众发起反核大示威。

  北京时间2011年3月11日13时46分，日本发生里氏8.9级地震，震源深度20千米。东京有强烈震感。地震引发10米高的海啸，并引发核电站爆炸。日本气象厅称这是世界观测史上最高震级的地震。日本"3·11大地震"造成的死亡和失踪人数达19867人，另有8.2万人前往避难所生活。半年来，福岛核危机处理仍在继续，核电站方圆20千米范围内上万名撤离的灾民至今还未能重返家园。日本新首相野田佳彦称"战斗才进行到一半，不平息核事故就不能恢复日本的信誉"。日本灾后恢复道路还十分遥远。

## An Anti-nuclear Protest in Japan

  In a country that has had almost no experience of mass protest since the 1960s, an unexpectedly large rally in Tokyo on September 19 against nuclear energy was a polished affair. As many as 60 000 people gathered on a public holiday in the city centre. They were given what could have been a menu of

lunch options for deciding on which route to march: the A-course, B-course or C-course, carefully chosen to avoid disrupting traffic. Musicians played and pet owners dressed their dogs in anti-nuclear vests. The only hint of menace was the number of people wearing face masks. But that was to keep off flu.

The Fukushima Dai-ichi nuclear-power plant remains unstable after the earthquake and tsunami of March 11, and 86 000 people from Fukushima prefecture are still unsure whether they will ever be able to return home because of the radiation fallout. So the demonstration might quite understandably have been an unruly affair. That it was not says a lot about Japan's curious attitude towards nuclear power—and towards protest. In general, say the organizers, people still prefer to be moderate rather than militant.

That is why, says Yasunari Fujimoto of an anti-nuclear group that planned the event, the demonstrators' demand is not to do away with nuclear power immediately, even though his organization favors that. An overhasty shutdown, he acknowledges, would cause electricity shortages and disrupt people's lives. Rather, the rally demanded the end of new construction and an agreed schedule for phasing out nuclear power. According to Mr. Fujimoto's models, the last existing nuclear plant could close down in 2049.

What is more, although the rally was against what Mr. Fujimoto calls a political cover-up of the danger of nuclear power, it was not, he stresses, anti-government. He has no issue with Japan's new prime minister, Yoshihiko Noda, even though Mr. Noda told the Wall Street Journal this week that it was "absolutely impossible" that Japan could get by without nuclear power next summer, and that there could be no quick phase-out of nuclear energy.

Mr. Fujimoto says Japan's way of protesting is different from the more hostile anti-nuclear rallies (which he attended) in Germany after Japan's March 11 disaster. "People in Japan like harmony," he says. "They tend to express themselves only after they know all the opinions." Masaru Tamamoto, an academic at Cambridge University, says mass protests last flourished after Japan's

American occupiers promoted unions and leftist parties in the wake of defeat in 1945. They quickly ebbed when Japanese conservatives suppressed the unions in the 1960s, and left-wing groups began to fight among themselves. Since then, there has been no group able to organize effective protest, Mr. Tamamoto points out.

An anti-nuclear coalition in Japan says it is trying to gather ten million signatures on a petition to submit to the government by the one-year anniversary of the accident at the Fukushima-1 nuclear power plant.

Protest organizers predicted 50 000 people would attend the event and say 60 000 actually participated.

Speaking at the rally, Nobel laureate Kenzaburo Oe called for Japan to follow an example set by Italy. In a general vote three months ago, 94 percent of Italian voters rejected a proposal to return to nuclear power generation.

Oe says Japanese need to fear the harmful physical effects of radiation caused by nuclear accidents as they did after the U.S. atomic bombings of Hiroshima and Nagasaki that ended the Second World War. He says rallies such as this one need to send a strong message to the government and business leaders of Japan.

Oe then helped lead part of the march, which organizers labeled as a "parade" rather than a demonstration.

Keiko Ochiai, a well-known feminist essayist, joined the Nobel laureate at the head of the march. She spoke with VOA news about her views on nuclear energy. "We believe that nuclear is the reason for the unhappiness of the human beings. So I can't agree with nuclear or nuclear plants itself," she said.

Recent polls indicate three-quarters of the public favor a gradual phase-out of nuclear power facilities in Japan, but only one in 10 Japanese want an immediate shutdown of all the plants in the country.

The March nuclear accident was the world's worst since the 1986 Chernobyl disaster in the former Soviet Union. The Fukushima radiation leaks forced

thousands of residents to abandon their homes and polluted crops and meat.

Japan has scant natural resources. That was the primary reason behind the push, over decades, to build nuclear plants and lessen the nation's reliance on imported fuel to generate electricity.

Japan's new Prime Minister, Yoshihiko Noda, appears to be moderating the stance of his predecessor, Naoto Kan, who was the country's leader at the start of the Fukushima crisis. According to the Kyodo news service, Noda is expected to tell a United Nations conference that Japan will continue to rely on nuclear plants while making safety at the facilities the top priority.

More than half of Japan's 52 nuclear reactors were offline, in recent months, leading to shortages of electricity. But conservation measures appear to have helped avoid feared blackouts.

## Notes

polished：精练的，文雅的，圆滑的
prefecture：管区，县
ebb：退潮，衰落
petition：请愿书，申请书，诉状
laureate：戴桂冠的人，获得者
scant：不足的，贫乏的

观察 OBSERVATION

# 日本上演反核游行

20世纪60年代以来,日本鲜有大规模群众抗议。9月19日,东京意外上演大规模反核能游行,场面温和克制。正值公共假日,市中心聚集了6万民众。大家可根据发放的类似午餐推荐的指南,决定其游行线路:A、B、C三条路线经过细心挑选,尽量减少对交通的阻碍。现场不仅有乐手演奏,还有宠物穿上了印有反核能标语的背心。唯一的威胁感来自若干戴口罩的民众,但他们只是为了防流感。

3月11日的地震和海啸过后,福岛一号核电站依然不稳定。由于核辐射,福岛县8.6万名居民仍不知道自己能否最终返回家园。所以,游行出现任何过激行为,都是可以理解的。游行未发生骚乱足以反映日本对核能乃至游行的微妙态度。组织者解释说,人们通常倾向于温和抗议,而非诉诸武力。

策划此次游行的是一个反核组织,其工作人员藤本康成表示,和平游行是因为示威者并不主张立刻废除核能,虽然组织方希望尽快。他认为,草率关停核电站会造成电力紧张,打乱民众生活。游行的目的是要求政府停止新核电站的建设,并出台逐步淘汰核能的时间表。根据藤本提供的模式,最后一个现存核电站可于2049年关闭。

此外,藤本强调,集会反对的是政府掩盖核事故的行为,而不是政府本身。尽管日本新首相野田佳彦在本周的《华尔街日报》中说日本没有核能"绝不可能"撑过明年夏天,且淘汰核能没有快速通道,但藤本对这位首相并不反感。

藤本说,日本的抗议方式与"3·11大地震"后的德国暴力反核集会

(他亲自参与)不同。"日本人民崇尚和平，"他说，"我们会在了解所有观点之后发表意见。"剑桥大学日籍学者玉本伟指出，1945年日本战败后，工会和左翼政党在美国的扶持下发展壮大，大规模抗议集会如雨后春笋般兴起。20世纪60年代，日本保守党开始镇压工会，群众游行迅速衰退，左翼团体内讧不断。藤本指出，日本从此再没有团体能组织起有效的抗议。

日本的一个反核联盟表示，他们正在为一份在福岛1号核电站事故发生一周年时准备递交给政府的请愿书，收集1千万人的签名。

游行活动的组织者本来预计，有5万人会参加抗议活动，现在他们表示，实际上有6万人参加。

诺贝尔奖获得者大江健三郎在集会上发表讲话，呼吁日本效仿意大利的先例。在三个月前举行的一次全民公决中，94%的意大利投票者拒绝一项重新开始核能发电的计划。

大江健三郎说，就像美国在广岛和长崎投放的两颗结束了二战的原子弹对日本人造成的伤害一样，日本人有理由对核事故造成的放射性污染对身体构成的有害影响感到害怕。他说，类似这次的集会需要向日本政府和商界领导人发出一个强有力的信息。

大江健三郎之后带头进行了部分游行活动。活动的组织者宣称这只是一场游行，而不是示威。

知名的女权主义随笔作家落合惠子也和诺贝尔奖得主大江健三郎一起走在游行队伍的最前面。她向美国之音讲述了她对核能的看法。她说："我们认为核能是造成人类痛苦的原因。所以我无法认同核能或者核电站。"

最近的民调显示，四分之三的公众赞成逐渐停用日本的核电设施，但是只有十分之一的日本人希望立即关闭全国所有的核电站。

2011年3月的核事故是自从前苏联1986年发生的切尔诺贝利灾难之后，全世界发生的最严重的核事故。福岛的辐射泄漏迫使成千上万居民放弃他们的家园以及受到污染的庄稼和肉类。

日本自然资源缺乏。这是几十年来推动建设核电厂，减少该国对进口发电燃料依赖的背后主要原因。

观察 OBSERVATION

日本新任首相野田佳彦看来在弱化他的前任菅直人的立场。菅直人在福岛危机发生时任日本首相。根据日本共同社报导,野田佳彦预计在联合国的一次会议上表明,日本将继续依靠核电厂,同时把保持核电设施的安全当作重中之重。

最近几个月来,日本52座核反应堆当中,有超过一半停机,导致日本电力短缺。但是节能措施看来帮助避免了人们所担心的停电现象。

**More to Read**

日本是一个资源相当匮乏的国家。因此,发展核能源成为了当初日本人一致支持的选择。在过去的宣传中,核能是清洁、安全、环保的代名词。即便当年的切尔诺贝利核泄漏事故也被认为是由于人为操作违反规程造成的。然而,随着"3·11大地震",日本认识到,核能远远没有之前宣传中所说的那么安全可靠。因而,从日本开始,反核运动蔓延到了中国台湾以及欧洲等核电大户。德国、荷兰等国已经宣布停建核电站。故事发生到这里,似乎核电已经成为了明日黄花。但且慢,欧洲国家的停建却并非仅仅因为日本核事故——德国在可再生能源技术方面已经取得突破,荷兰等国则具有丰富的水力和风力资源。这些都是日本无法比拟的。因此,除非你愿意和所有电器说拜拜,否则废弃核能在日本并不像很多人想象的那样板上钉钉。

## Reading Guidance

2011年9月17日起,美国纽约爆发一场名为"占领华尔街"的民众抗议活动,并一直持续到10月份。"占领华尔街"抗议活动的矛头主要指向华尔街"贪婪"、金融系统弊病和政府监管不力,以及美国政府过度动用军力、对少数族裔不公、失业率高等社会问题。此后,这股抗议浪潮开始向美国其他城市蔓延,其中,洛杉矶、波士顿、芝加哥、丹佛和西雅图都发生了抗议活动。10月1日,美国的阿尔布开克、新墨西哥、波士顿和洛杉矶也爆发了游行示威。10月2日,超过500名的洛杉矶民众在洛杉矶市政厅前的草坪安营扎寨,开始示威抗议活动,并效仿纽约"占领华尔街"的示威活动,打出"占领洛杉矶"的口号。有分析人士称,"占领华尔街"示威行动,反映了美国经济困境下经济、社会矛盾加剧,更表明金融危机以来美国政府和监管当局推出经济、金融改革措施未孚众望。

# Wall Street Protests Continue And Grow Across the Country

NEW YORK—Protesters speaking out against corporate greed and other issues showed no signs of giving up their campaign on Monday, with organizers urging participants to dress up as corporate zombies and to take part in a rally against police brutality.

The arrests of 700 people on Brooklyn Bridge over the weekend fueled the anger of the protesters camping in a Manhattan park and sparked support elsewhere in the country as the campaign entered its third week.

Occupy Wall Street started with fewer than a dozen college students spending days and nights in Zuccotti Park, a plaza near the city's financial center. But a day after Saturday's mass arrests, hundreds of protesters were resolute and like-minded groups in other cities had joined in.

Group spokesman Patrick Bruner urged protesters on Monday to dress up as corporate zombies and eat Monopoly money to let financial workers "see us reflecting the metaphor of their actions."

As the encampment slowly began waking up Monday morning, several dozen police officers stood in formation across the street.

One camper set up a table with tubes of makeup and stacks of fake money and was applying white makeup to the face of a young woman.

John Hildebrand, 24, an unemployed teacher from Norman, Oklahoma, sat up in his sleeping bag around 10 a.m.. He said he arrived Saturday after getting a cheap plane ticket to New York.

"My issue is corporate influence in politics," he said. "I would like to eliminate corporate financing from politics."

He said he was returning home on Tuesday and planned to organize a similar protest there.

One supporter, William Stack, sent an email to city officials urging that all charges be dropped against those arrested.

"It is not a crime to demand that our money be spent on meeting people's needs, not for massive corporate bailouts," he wrote. "The real criminals are in the boardrooms and executive offices on Wall Street, not the people marching for jobs and health care."

Police said the department will continue its regular patrols of the area. And "as always, if it is a lawful demonstration, we help facilitate and if they break the law we arrest them," NYPD spokesman Paul Browne said.

Wiljago Cook, 33, of Oakland, California, who joined the protest on the first day, said "exposing police brutality wasn't even really on my agenda but my eyes have been opened."

She and her boyfriend and two neighbors all quit their jobs to come and planned "to stay as long as it seems useful," said Cook, who had worked for a nonprofit theater group.

She was wearing zombie makeup that included a red streak down her forehead. "It's a cheeky and fun way to make the same point that we've been making," Cook said of her painted face.

A map of the country displayed on the plaza identified 21 places where other protests were organized.

Wall-Street style demonstrations with names like Occupy Los Angeles, Occupy Chicago, and Occupy Boston were staged in front of Federal Reserve buildings in those cities. A group in Columbus, Ohio, also marched on the capital city's street. And signs of support were rearing up outside the U.S. In Canada, a Wall Street rally is planned for later this month in Toronto.

"It was chaos here." two weeks ago, said Jackie Fellner, a marketing manager from Westchester County, north of the city.

Campers take turns organizing a "general assembly" on the plaza where they divide tasks among themselves. They have "a protocol for most things", said 19-year-old Kira Moyer-Sims of Portland, Oregon, including a makeshift hospital and getting legal help for people who are arrested. They rally around a website, and they even started printing a newspaper—*The Occupied Wall Street Journal*.

The campers also have been fueled by encouraging words from well-known figures, the latest actor Alec Baldwin, who posted videos that had already been widely circulated. One appeared to show police using pepper spray on a group of women, another young man being tackled to the ground by an officer.

"This is unsettling," Baldwin wrote. "I think the NYPD has a PR problem."

Fellner said she has an issue with "big money dictating which politicians get elected and what programs get funded".

But "we're not here to take down Wall Street," she insisted. "It's not poor against rich".

Still, the protesters chose Wall Street as their physical rallying point, speaking against corporate greed, social inequality, global climate change and other concerns.

Beside the mass arrest Saturday, police arrested about 100 people Sept. 24 when protesters marched to other parts of the city and got into a tense standoff with officers.

Some said protesters on the Brooklyn Bridge were lured onto the roadway by police, or they didn't hear the calls from authorities to head to the pedestrian walkway. Police said no one was tricked into being arrested, and that those in the back of the group who couldn't hear were allowed to leave.

The NYPD released video footage Sunday to back up its stance. In one of the videos, an official uses a bullhorn to warn the crowd. Marchers can be seen chanting, "Take the bridge."

## Notes

rally: 集会
plaza: 广场
encampment: 设营;野营
NYPD: New York Police Department, 纽约市警察局
tackle: 对付;交涉
chant: 叫喊

# 华尔街抗议活动仍在继续，并向全美蔓延

纽约——抗议者高呼反对企业贪婪和其他不满，星期一还没有迹象表明他们会放弃示威游行。抗议组织者号召大家打扮成企业僵尸的模样并参加抗议警察暴行的集会。

上周末布鲁克林桥上700人被捕令曼哈顿公园露营的抗议者火上浇油，并且引发了美国其他城市的声援。至此，抗议活动进入第三周。

"占领华尔街"运动起初只不过是十几个大学生在纽约金融中心附近的一个广场祖科蒂公园日夜露营活动。但星期六的大规模逮捕发生之后的第二天，成千上万的抗议者毅然决然地走上街头，还有其他城市的类似组织也纷纷加入其中。

星期一，占领华尔街组织的发言人帕特里克·布鲁纳号召示威者打扮成吞噬垄断财富的企业僵尸，让金融界人士"看到我们在如何暗讽他们的所作所为"。

星期一的早上，当露营的示威者逐渐醒来，大家发现街对面列队站立着数十个警察。

一个宿营者架起桌子，摆好化妆用的颜料和一堆一堆的假钱，正准备把一个年轻女孩的脸化妆成白色。

约翰·希尔德布兰德，24岁，是从俄克拉荷马州诺曼市来的一名失业教师。早上10点左右，他从睡袋里坐起。他说他买的是非常便宜的飞机票，星期六抵达纽约的。

"我的质疑是企业对政治的影响。"他说，"我希望政府不要对企业进行金融资助。"

观察 OBSERVATION

他说他打算星期二回家,并在当地组织类似的抗议活动。

声援者威廉·斯戴克给纽约市官员写了电子邮件,要求他们撤销对被逮捕者的所有指控。

"要求把国家的钱用来满足人民的需求,而不是用在数目庞大的企业援助上不是犯罪,"他在信中写道,"真正的罪犯在华尔街的董事会议上和行政办公室里,而不是为了争取工作和医疗保险而游行的人民。"

警方声称他们会继续该地区的日常巡逻。而且,"像往常一样,如果游行示威合法,我们会给予便利,但如果触犯法律,我们就要逮捕他们。"纽约警察局发言人保罗·布朗说。

第一天就加入抗议活动的威尔加戈·库克,33岁,来自加利福尼亚州的奥克兰。他说,"揭露警察的暴行原本不在我的日程当中,但是我可不能视而不见啊。"

库克原本在一个非营利的剧院集团工作。她和她的男朋友,还有两个邻居,都是辞掉了工作过来参加抗议的,打算"一直在这儿坚持到有所收获",库克说。

她打扮成了僵尸的样子,额头上还有一条红色血迹。库克提到自己的妆容时说,"这种搞笑的、放肆的方式正好契合我们所要表达的内容。"

广场上展示的一张美国地图上明确标注着其他21个组织了抗议活动的地点。

效仿华尔街抗议活动,示威者以诸如"占领洛杉矶""占领芝加哥""占领波士顿"之名聚集在各自城市的联邦储备银行大楼前。俄亥俄州的首府哥伦布市也有示威者上街游行。美国境外也出现了声援的迹象。加拿大多伦多的反华尔街集会计划于10月份末举行。

纽约市北部威斯特彻斯特县的一名市场销售经理杰吉·费尔纳两个星期前就觉得"这里够混乱的了"。

现在露营者在广场轮流组织"大会",并给他们自己分配任务。来自俄勒冈州波特兰19岁的吉拉·莫亚尔—希姆斯介绍说,他们制定了"一个总体协议",包括临时医院和对被逮捕人员的法律支援。而且他们还在网站上集会,甚至开始印刷报纸——《被占领的华尔街日报》。

露营者也能从知名人物那里得到响应和鼓舞。新星艾力克·鲍德温上传的视频已被广为流传。视频里警方使用胡椒喷雾在喷射一群女性,另一位年轻人则被警察按在地上。

"我认为纽约警察局存在公关问题。"鲍德温写道,"这很让人担心。"

费尔纳觉得问题在于"(华尔街的)巨额财富会左右政治选举和国家项目资金"。

但是"我们到这儿来不是为了扳倒华尔街",她坚持说道,"这不是穷人对富人的战争。"

但抗议者仍然选择华尔街作为集会地点,来反对企业的贪婪,社会的不公平,全球气候变化和其他社会问题。

不光是星期六布鲁克林大桥的大规模逮捕行为,9月24警方还在城市其他地区逮捕了约100名示威者。抗议活动陷入与警方对峙的僵局。

有人认为,布鲁克林大桥上的抗议者是被警察误引到机动车道的,也有可能他们没有听到警方要求大家沿人行道行进。警方称,不存在诱捕,那些在行进队伍后面没有听见命令的人后来被释放。

星期日,纽约警察局公布录像片断来表明立场。在其中的一个视频里,一名警员使用扩音器警告抗议人群,游行者们则高喊口号"拿下布鲁克林桥"。

---

## More to Read

如今,美国人生活成本、居住成本、出行成本、教育成本都在上升,这势必会激化社会矛盾。这种现象可谓"金融危机后遗症"。美国的经济问题在很大程度上反映了政治问题。这次游行反映了美国社会在分裂,不仅表现为国会两党在诸多问题上的分歧在加大,还表现为美国社会群体的两极化。但这种危机的显现并不代表美国的经济走向低谷,更不能说明美国的实力已经衰弱。群众抗议正是美国国内纠错机制的一种表现,通过不同利益群体发出自己的声音,美国在政策上必然会做出一定的回应和调整。这恰恰是美国实力能够经久不衰的重要条件。

观 察 OBSERVATION

## Reading Guidance

　　美国加利福尼亚州长杰里·布朗于2011年10月7日签署一项法案,禁止在加州出售、经销和持有鱼翅。该法案规定,自2013年1月1日起,加州禁止进口鱼翅。这意味着加州这个美国境内鱼翅消费量最大的区域,通过立法将完全禁止鱼翅交易活动。市场上1磅鱼翅售价超过600美元,而1磅鲨鱼肉不到1美元。由于鲨鱼肉几乎没有商业价值,渔民经常在割掉鲨鱼的鳍后,将鲨鱼扔回大海,任凭其死去。如果全球对鱼翅需求量不减少,将会导致鲨鱼大量消失,这将给海洋生物多样性、食品安全带来灾难性影响。为保护野生鲨鱼资源,美国夏威夷、俄勒冈和华盛顿州此前已通过有关禁止鱼翅的法律。

　　鱼翅是鲨鱼鳍,在亚洲的饮食文化中常被看成是珍贵的菜肴。不过,专家认为鱼翅并没有特别的营养,一碗鸡汤所含的脂肪、钙、碳水化合物、蛋白质和能量要多于等量的鱼翅。

　　但是,此项法案自提出后在加州华裔社区引起强烈反响,政界、业界和普通民众表现出两极分化的态度。

# California Bans Shark Fin

People in California can no longer eat the Chinese delicacy of shark fin

soup. The Governor of California officially made it illegal to sell or possess shark fin. The ban is a part of a growing movement worldwide to save the shark population. But there are some Chinese who feel California's ban on shark fin is unfair and discriminatory.

Shark fin soup is a delicacy in Chinese cooking that dates back hundreds of years. The expensive dish has become increasingly popular as more Chinese are getting wealthy. But conservationists, like Sarah Sikich of Heal the Bay, say the demand for shark fin is devastating the shark population.

Sikich says the practice of finning is popular among fishermen who would catch the shark, slice off the fin and throw the fish back into the ocean to die.

Barbara Long at the Aquarium of the Pacific says when the shark population is put at risk; the health of the ocean is also in danger. "Sharks are a top predator and play a very vital role in marine ecosystems," said Long.

Celebrities like Chinese basketball star Yao Ming and British tycoon Richard Branson are asking the Chinese to stop eating shark fin soup. U.S. law requires all sharks that are brought on shore to have their fins attached. California now joins three other U.S. states for even stricter regulations that ban the sale of shark fin, a commodity that is worth as much as $700 a kilogram.

Basketball superstar Yao Ming and British entrepreneur Richard Branson joined forces last month to get shark fin soup off the menu and save some of the species from extinction.

The soup, considered a delicacy, is widely served at top-class restaurants on the mainland, Hong Kong and Taiwan. To cater for demand about 1.5 million sharks are slaughtered every week for their fins, a move that endangers some species.

"Few people know the importance of sharks in maintaining the ecological balance," recently retired NBA star Yao said in Shanghai during an event, sponsored by conservation group WildAid, to launch the campaign against the shark fin trade.

WildAid, which seeks to halt the trade in wildlife, estimates up to 73 million sharks are harvested annually, mainly for shark fin soup. The campaign, launched in Shanghai, also released a website for people to make an online pledge to stop eating the soup, said the organizer of WildAid.

Yao, who retired from the sport in July but remains one of China's biggest sporting names, made a pledge to stop eating shark fin soup five years ago and has since served as an ambassador for WildAid.

"Nor do they realize the cruelty of the finning process," Yao said. "There is no reasonable explanation for the cruelty." After the fins are sliced off, sharks are discarded back to the ocean where they are condemned to a slow, agonizing death due to diminished speed and maneuverability.

Despite growing calls to ban the trade and consumption of shark products, demand in China has been growing rapidly as the economy booms.

"Those who eat shark fin soup told me they don't particularly like it," Branson, president of Virgin Atlantic Airlines, said. "It was just the tradition. That means it's possible to get people to switch to other food, and make the soup unfashionable." "I simply cannot imagine a world without sharks – we must not let this happen," he said in the statement.

"Because the fin is driving the market value of the shark, it's most important to target that aspect. California is the leading importer of shark fin to the U.S. It's estimated that 85 percent of the shark fin that enters the U.S. comes through California." Noted Sikich.

But opponents of the California ban say the law unfairly targets the Chinese community because it only bans shark fin and not the entire shark. California State Senator Ted Lieu voted against the ban.

"You can slaughter this highly vulnerable shark for fish and chips, but a Chinese restaurant couldn't take a shark fin from one of the hundreds of shark species which are nowhere near endangered and to me that is completely discriminatory and very unfair," said Lieu.

Many opponents of the shark fin ban say they would support a ban on the entire shark. That's exactly what eight representatives ranging from Latin American countries to Micronesia have pledged. They signed a declaration at the United Nations to develop shark sanctuaries that would end the commercial fishing of sharks.

## Notes

discriminatory：歧视的，差别待遇的
conservationist：自然资源保护论者，自然资源保护学家
predator：食肉动物；掠夺者
tycoon：有钱有势的企业家，大亨
discard：丢弃，抛弃
maneuverability：可操作性，机动性
sanctuary：庇护所，避难所

# 美国加州颁布"鱼翅"禁令

美国加利福尼亚州的人们不能再吃鱼翅汤这种中餐佳肴了。加州州长正式宣布，销售或拥有鲨鱼鳍是非法行为。这项禁令是在全球范围内日益增长的拯救鲨鱼运动的一部分。然而，一些华人感到，加州这项禁令不但不公平，而且还具有歧视性。

鱼翅汤是中国烹调的一种美味佳肴，它的历史可以追溯到几百年前。由于中国人越来越富有，因此，这道昂贵的菜也越来越受欢迎。可是，诸如

环保组织"治愈湾区"的萨拉·希基赫这样的自然资源保护主义者表示,对鱼翅汤的大量需求正在毁灭鲨鱼种群。

希基赫说,切除鱼鳍的做法在渔民中很普遍,他们捕捉到鲨鱼后把鱼鳍割下来,随后就把鲨鱼扔回大海,任由其死去。

太平洋水族馆的芭芭拉·朗说,当鲨鱼种群面临风险时,太平洋的状况也会处于危险之中。"鲨鱼是海洋中最凶猛的食肉动物,它在海洋生态系统中具有极其重要的作用。"她说道。

像中国篮球明星姚明和英国亿万富翁理查德·布兰森这样的名人都呼吁华人不要食用鱼翅汤。美国法律要求所有被捕捉上岸的鲨鱼都要有完整的鱼鳍。加州现在也加入到另外三个州的行列,做出了更为严格的规定——禁止销售鲨鱼鳍。鲨鱼鳍的商品价值高达每千克700美元。

篮球明星姚明和英国企业家理查德·布兰森爵士上个月共同出席活动,倡导和呼吁人们拒绝食用鱼翅,拯救濒临灭绝的鲨鱼。

鱼翅由于其味道鲜美,在中国大陆、香港和台湾等地的高级饭店里被广泛食用。为了迎合消费需求,每星期有150万只鲨鱼被切下鱼鳍而死,这一现象使得许多鲨鱼种类已经濒临灭绝。

近期退役的NBA球星姚明在活动现场表示,"很少人知道鲨鱼在保持生态平衡中的重要作用"。此次由国际环保组织野生动物救援协会在上海举行的活动,目的是为了发起抵制鱼翅贸易行动。

野生动物救援协会力求停止一切野生动物的贸易活动。据他们估计,每年有多达7300万只鲨鱼被捕杀,主要用于鱼翅汤。野生动物救援协会的组织者说,在上海举行的这次活动还发布了一个网站,大家可以在线做出承诺拒绝食用鱼翅汤。

姚明虽然已于今年7月退役,但他仍然是中国体育界响当当的体育明星之一。姚明在五年前宣布拒绝食用鱼翅汤,从那之后他一直担当野生动物救援协会的大使至今。

姚明表示:"很少有人知道鲨鱼被切下鱼鳍的过程有多残忍。"他还说,"对于这样的残忍,根本就不存在合理的解释。"鲨鱼的鱼鳍被切下来之后,就被遗弃扔回大海。没有了鱼鳍,它们的速度和灵活性会降低,只能痛苦地、漫长地等待死亡的来临。

尽管呼吁禁止鲨鱼产品贸易和消费的呼声持续不断，但随着中国经济的迅猛发展，中国社会上对鱼翅的需求也在迅速增加。

维珍大西洋航空创始人布兰森表示，"那些吃过鱼翅的人跟他说他们也并没有很爱吃，只是传统而已。这也就意味着，可以让人们改成吃别的，让鱼翅汤不再被追捧。"他还说"我就是没办法想象没有鲨鱼的世界——我们绝不能让它发生"。

希基赫说："因为鲨鱼鳍推动着鲨鱼的市场价值，因此，重要的是把控制目标对准鲨鱼鳍。加州是美国进口鲨鱼鳍的主要地点。据估计，进入美国的鲨鱼鳍中，有85%是经由加州进口的。"

可是，反对加州这项禁令的人士说，这项法律不公平地把打击目标对准华人社区，因为该法律只是禁止鲨鱼鳍而并未禁止整条鲨鱼。加州的华裔州参议员刘云平投票反对这项禁令。

刘云平说："你们为了炸鱼薯条可以屠宰极易受到攻击的鲨鱼，而中餐馆却不能从一种鲨鱼身上提取鱼鳍，而且这种鲨鱼是几百种完全没有灭绝危险的鲨鱼种群的一种。我认为，这是完全歧视华人的禁令，也是很不公平的。"

鲨鱼鳍禁令的许多反对者说，他们愿意支持一项不许捕捉整条鲨鱼的禁令。这恰恰是来自拉美国家和西太平洋岛群密克罗尼西亚的8个代表已经做出的保证。他们在联合国签署了一项宣言，要开发一个鲨鱼保护区，结束商业捕捉鲨鱼。

**More to Read**

　　当不同文化遭遇时,许多原本在各自文化中理所当然的事情就变得很可疑了。对于中国人来讲,鱼翅燕窝的美食自古有之。人们在品尝美味佳肴时并不会将碗中的"食材"同残忍杀戮、生态平衡等问题联系在一起。然而,随着媒体的报道和名人做出的示范,越来越多的人已经意识到吃鱼翅并不是什么太值得骄傲的事情。在这一问题上,生态平衡(即生存)的价值要超越文化的价值。另一方面,以法令的形式规定销售或拥有鲨鱼鳍是非法行为当然是从制度层面上保证生态平衡,仅就这一点而言也是值得嘉许的。不过,正如许多批评者提到的那样,只禁鱼翅而不禁捕鲨的做法会带给人们很多在文化歧视方面的负面联想——这种做法本身也让人略感荒唐。如今,包装在科学话语(也包括自由主义意识形态)之下的中西方文化冲突(也不限于文化)是一种新的现象,很值得深入思考。

 Reading Guidance

10月4日,2011年诺贝尔物理学奖揭晓,三位美国科学家折桂。今年诺贝尔物理学奖得主的成就与整个宇宙相关,三名获奖者依靠观测遥远的超新星,发现宇宙正在加速膨胀,而且逐渐变冷,最后包括地球在内的整个宇宙将会变成冰。1929年,美国天文学家哈勃首先发现了星体间距离不断变大的现象,并提出宇宙膨胀理论。这一发现导致俄裔美国天体物理学家伽莫夫提出"大爆炸理论",他认为,我们的宇宙诞生于约140亿年前的一次大爆炸,在大爆炸之前,宇宙是个极小体积、极高密度的点,而大爆炸之后,宇宙不断膨胀。多年来,天体物理学界一直认为宇宙是在以一个恒定的速度膨胀,直到这三位科学家开始了对超新星的观测。珀尔马特与施密特分别于1988年和1994年开始领导各自团队从事超新星研究,里斯在施密特的团队中发挥了重要作用。两个研究小组于1998年得到了一致的结论:宇宙的膨胀速度不是恒定的,也不是越来越慢,而是不断加快。这项成果堪称宇宙探索道路上的里程碑。瑞典皇家科学院称该发现"震动了宇宙学的基础"。

# Three Americans Share 2011 Nobel Prize in Physics

Three U. S. -born scientists won the Nobel Prize in physics Tuesday for discovering that the universe is expanding at an accelerating pace, a stunning revelation that suggests the cosmos will eventually freeze to ice.

The Royal Swedish Academy of Sciences says American Saul Perlmutter, U.S.-Australian citizen Brian Schmidt and U.S. scientist Adam Riess share the 2011 Nobel Prize in physics. The trio were honored Tuesday, Oct. 4, 2011 "for the discovery of the accelerating expansion of the universe through observations of distant supernovae."

The Royal Swedish Academy of Sciences said the prize winners would share the 10 million kronor ($1.5 million) award. Half of the prize money went to the U.S. physicist Saul Perlmutter and the other half to the US-born researcher Brian Schmidt who is based in Australia, and another U.S. scientist, Adam Riess. The award was greeted with widespread approval from scientists, though some argued that by recognizing only three physicists, the prize distorted how the research was done.

Working in two separate research teams during the 1990s—Perlmutter in one and Schmidt and Riess in the other—the scientists raced to map the universe's expansion by analyzing a particular type of supernovas, or exploding stars.

They found that the light emitted by more than 50 distant supernovas was weaker than expected, a sign that the universe was expanding at an accelerating rate, the academy said.

"For almost a century the universe has been known to be expanding as a consequence of the Big Bang about 14 billion years ago," the citation said. "However the discovery that this expansion is accelerating is astounding. If the expansion will continue to speed up the universe will end in ice."

The discovery in the late 1990s meant textbooks had to be rewritten and forced researchers to consider a universe of stars and planets that is being torn apart by a mysterious force that counteracts gravity.

Perlmutter, 52, heads the Supernova Cosmology Project at the Lawrence Berkeley National Laboratory and University of California, Berkeley.

Schmidt, 44, is the head of the High-z Supernova Search Team at the Australian National University.

Riess, 41, is an astronomy professor at Johns Hopkins University and Space Telescope Science Institute in Baltimore, Maryland.

Schmidt said he was just sitting down to have dinner with his family in Canberra, Australia, when the phone call came. "I was somewhat suspicious when the Swedish voice came on," Schmidt told The Associated Press. "My knees sort of went weak and I had to walk around and sort my senses out."

The academy said the three researchers were stunned by their own discoveries—they had expected to find that the expansion of the universe was slowing down. But both teams reached the opposite conclusion: faraway galaxies were racing away from each other at an ever-increasing speed.

The discovery was "the biggest shakeup in physics, in my opinion, in the last 30 years," said Phillip Schewe, a physicist and spokesman at the Joint Quantum Institute, which is operated by the University of Maryland and the federal government.

"I remember everyone thinking at the time (that) there was some mistake," Schewe said. But there was no mistake, and in fact the basic finding was confirmed later by other measurements. Other scientists found evidence for it when they analyzed the microwave radiation left over from the big bang that still bathes the universe, he said.

Perlmutter told AP his team made the discovery in steps, analyzing the data and assuming it was wrong. "And after months, you finally believe it," he said. "It's not quite a surprise anymore. I tell people it's the longest 'ah-ha' experience that you've ever had."

An accelerating universe means it will get increasingly colder as matter is spread out across ever-vaster distances in space, said the Nobel physics committee. The acceleration is believed to be driven by an unknown cosmic power, called dark energy, one of the great mysteries of the universe.

观 察 OBSERVATION

Fred Dylla, executive director of the American Institute of Physics, said the prize confirmed an idea from Albert Einstein, called the cosmological constant, that Einstein inserted in his general theory of relativity, a cornerstone of modern physics.

Einstein later denied that idea as his "biggest blunder," but it did lead to a lot of theoretical and experimental studies, Dylla said.

The research implies that billions of years from now, the universe will become "a very, very large, but very cold and lonely place," said Charles Blue, spokesman for the American Institute of Physics.

In contrast to the big bang, that fate has been called the "big rip" to indicate how galaxies would be torn apart, he said. Galaxies will be flying away so quickly that their light could not travel across the universe to distant observers as it does today, making the sky appears black, he said.

"The Nobel committee's comment that the universe would end in ice is an eloquent way of putting it." Blue said.

## Notes

revelation: (惊人的)新发现;揭示
cosmos: 宇宙
supernovae: 超新星
counteract: 对……起反作用,抵消
cornerstone: 奠基石
blunder: 错误

# 三位美国科学家分享2011年诺贝尔物理学奖

　　三位美国科学家于本周二荣获诺贝尔物理学奖。他们发现宇宙正在加速膨胀，这一惊人的发现说明宇宙最终将变成冰。

　　瑞典皇家科学院宣布将2011年诺贝尔物理学奖授予美国科学家索尔·珀尔马特、拥有美国和澳大利亚双重国籍的科学家布赖恩·施密特以及美国科学家亚当·里斯。2011年10月4日，三位科学家凭借观测遥远的超新星发现了宇宙正在加速扩张而一起问鼎诺贝尔奖。

　　瑞典皇家科学院宣布三位获奖者分享1000万瑞典克朗（约合150万美元）的奖金。美国物理学家索尔·珀尔马特获得其中的一半，居住在澳大利亚的美籍研究者布赖恩·施密特和另一位美国科学家亚当·里斯分享另一半。他们的获奖受到学界的广泛认可，但是也有人质疑奖项仅仅颁给三位物理学家是抹杀了研究的过程。

　　20世纪90年代，珀尔马特和施密特、里斯分处两个不同的研究团队。但这三位科学家都致力于通过分析一种特殊的超新星（爆炸恒星）来探测宇宙的膨胀。

　　瑞典皇家科学院说，科学家们发现50多个遥远的超新星所发出的光比预想的要微弱得多，这就表明宇宙正在加速膨胀。

　　"近一个世纪以来，公认的看法是，大约140亿年前的大爆炸之后宇宙一直在膨胀。"评审委员会说。"然而，发现宇宙的膨胀正在加速着实令人震惊。如果这种膨胀继续加速的话，宇宙将以冰冻状态终结。"

　　上个世纪末的这一发现意味着教科书必须改写，研究者们必须相信诸多星球组成的宇宙正在被一种能够抵消地心引力的神秘力量撕扯。

观察 OBSERVATION

珀尔马特,今年52岁,是美国加州大学伯克利分校、劳伦斯—伯克利国家实验室超新星宇宙项目的负责人。

施密特,今年44岁,是澳大利亚国立大学"高红移超新星搜寻团队"的负责人。

里斯,今年41岁,是美国约翰霍普金斯大学和太空望远镜科学学会(位于马里兰州巴尔的摩市)的天文学教授。

施密特说,当电话铃响的时候,他正和家人在澳大利亚堪培拉的家里坐享晚餐。"当听到来自瑞典的声音,我真的不敢相信。"施密特告诉美联社说,"我两腿发软,走了几步之后,才回过神来。"

瑞典皇家科学院说,三位研究者对于自己的发现都很惊讶。他们原本以为研究结果会是宇宙的膨胀速度在减慢。但是,两个研究团队都得到了与预期相反的结论:遥远的星系正在以前所未有的加速度彼此远离。

菲利普·舍韦说,"在我看来,这是近30年里最震撼物理学界的发现。"菲利普·舍韦是美国联邦政府和马里兰州立大学共同管理的美国联合量子学院的物理学家和发言人。

舍韦说,"我记得那个时候所有人都在想这个发现一定有问题。"他还说,但的确没有任何问题,事实上这一发现很快就得到其他测量方法的证实。其他的科学家们分析了大爆炸之后遗留下来并笼罩宇宙的微波辐射,从中也得到有力证据。

珀尔马特告诉美联社说,他的研究团队得到这一发现的过程非常谨慎,在研究中他们分析数据,曾经认为它是错误的结果。"几个月之后,你终于相信了。"他说,"这不再是令人吃惊的事。我和我的队员说,这是你们所经历过的最为漫长的等待惊喜的过程。"

诺贝尔物理委员会说,加速膨胀的宇宙意味着,随着宇宙中的物质在前所未有的浩瀚空间中存在,宇宙将加速变冷。科学家们认为宇宙加速膨胀的动力来源于一种叫暗能量的未知宇宙力量,这也是宇宙未解之谜之一。

美国物理协会的执行理事弗雷德·戴勒说,今年的诺贝尔奖肯定了爱因斯坦引入到相对论的宇宙学常数,这是现代物理学的奠基石。

爱因斯坦曾经自己否定了宇宙学常数的观点,认为是他一生中所犯的最大错误。但是,它的确引发了大量的理论研究和实验研究。戴勒说。

这项研究表明,亿万年之后的宇宙将变成一个"非常广袤、非常冰冷的孤独世界"。美国物理协会的发言人查尔斯·布鲁说。

他说,相对于大爆炸,星系将被撕裂的未来被称作"大撕裂"。他还说,星系间快速飞离彼此,它们所发出的光不能穿过宇宙,到那时,作为遥远观察者的我们就不能像现在这样看到它们的光,所以天空将一片黑暗。

"诺贝尔奖委员会所谓'宇宙将最终冻结成冰'的说法是对这一现象的清楚描述。"布鲁说。

### More to Read

诺贝尔科学奖堪称人类智慧的集大成者,其得主毫无疑问都属于最聪明的那些科学家。但我们也发现,这些最聪明的人所从事的研究大都是基础性和前沿性的,往往无法在短期内变成专利、产生"效益",而一项科学成果被诺贝尔奖承认也需要经过多年的沉淀和检验。总而言之,诺贝尔奖是"急不来"的。随着中国国力增强和科研事业的迅速发展,人们目前都在预测,中国本土的科学家什么时候可以获奖。中国的研究者其实是有潜力的,不久前获得美国医药学界最高奖拉斯克奖的屠呦呦教授即是最佳例证。他们现在需要的不仅是充足的经费和先进的设备,可能还需要良好的科研环境和那么一点点耐心。

观察 OBSERVATION

**Reading Guidance**

俄罗斯总理普京于 2011 年 10 月 6 日在莫斯科表示,俄罗斯不会放弃加入世界贸易组织的目标,但入世前提是相关方面没有提出令俄方无法接受的条件。俄罗斯 1993 年正式申请加入关税与贸易总协定(世贸组织前身),1995 年正式开始入世谈判。作为最后一个仍未加入世贸组织的重要经济体,俄罗斯希望能在今年年底前加入世贸组织,俄政府将此列为其核心任务之一。不过,俄罗斯经济发展部长纳比乌林娜 9 月中旬表示,俄罗斯入世谈判还存在一些难以逾越的障碍,要想按原计划于今年年底加入世贸组织可能性不大。10 月 8 日,格鲁吉亚与宿敌俄罗斯就俄入世问题进行的谈判在未达成协议的情况下结束。格鲁吉亚说,它会阻挠俄罗斯入世,除非莫斯科改变立场。由于世贸组织成员国必须一致同意才能做出决定,格鲁吉亚对俄罗斯成为世贸组织成员国握有否决权。

# Putin Urges Choice on Admitting Russia to World Trade Organization

Russia's principal trading partners should decide soon whether to admit Russia to the World Trade Organization, Prime Minister Vladimir V. Putin said in his first direct address to investors after announcing that he would run again for president next year.

Russia's membership application to the trade group has been 18 years until now. But this week, officials in both the United States and Russia suggested that Russia, which is by far the largest economy still outside the WTO, was close to membership.

Referring to the current obstacles to Russia's accession to the WTO, Putin said, in general, Russia and the United States and Europe have been assembled on the Russia automobile industry and agricultural subsidies and other issues basically reached a consensus, but the unresolved relationship with Georgia.

One remaining obstacle is a demand by Georgia, a member of the organization, that international monitors be positioned at customs clearance points between Russia and two separatist regions, Abkhazia and South Ossetia. Russia, which largely controls the regions but officially considers them independent nations, has rejected monitors.

Because accepting new nations in the WTO is generally decided by consensus among the members, now numbering 153 states, Georgia has wound up with exceptional leverage.

Russia has been applying to join the organization since 1993, when the group was called the General Agreement on Tariffs and Trade. But a series of disputes over airplane tariffs, international trade in chickens and allegations that Russia has allowed abuse of intellectual property rights has repeatedly blocked its membership. Russia's WTO negotiators appear to have removed most of the remaining obstacles to accession; it emerged this week, including differences on meat imports, sanitary standards and incentives to Russian automobile producers. The World Bank says Russia's economy will benefit by joining, as will companies that export goods to Russia.

Mr. Putin attended the third "Russia calls" Investment Forum in Moscow, sponsored by the state bank VTB and said the need for Russia's WTO accession on the issue remains controversial in the Russian business community. "Russian accession to the WTO shares pros and cons, but overall, the benefit is

## 观察 OBSERVATION

greater than disadvantages. Russia's WTO accession will not give up goals on the premise that Russia does not make unacceptable conditions."

"I have a question." Mr. Putin said in remarks at the Forum.

"Do our main partners in Europe and the United States want Russia to become a WTO member or not?" he asked. "There is no need to take refuge in the Georgia issue. If they want, they can have this very quickly, especially considering that we have reached a compromise on most issues." In the speech, Mr. Putin said he did not expect the global economy to dip into a second recession, something that could disproportionately affect Russia because of its dependence on oil exports.

In addition, Vladimir Putin earlier told reporters that although the euro zone sovereign debt crisis faced by some countries, but he has confidence in the euro. Putin added, "The establishment of a good relationship between Russia and the European is inevitable."

In a comment apparently intended to ease the financial community's concerns about investing in Russia, Mr. Putin said that the widely admired former finance minister, Aleksei L. Kudrin, who was fired last month, would remain a "member of our team." He said, "We will be working with him." without specifying any position he might have.

Igor I. Shuvalov, a Russian deputy prime minister, said Tuesday after a visit to Washington that American trade negotiators were now advocating Russia's membership with other nations. They are working "24 hours a day" to persuade other WTO members to accept Russia's application. The nearly two-decade-long process, he said, is "very close" to completion.

But Mr. Putin said that the United States and Europe had asked Russia to negotiate a settlement with Georgia. Mr. Putin said the countries were no closer to a compromise today than when talks began in March.

The trade organization negotiations have taken on some added significance as a measure of how the world will react to Mr. Putin's decision, announced

late last month, to seek another term as president. Mr. Putin's comments suggested he expected the United States and Europe to pressure Georgia to accede to Russian membership in the organization.

Georgia's president has said it is in his country's interest for Russia to join the WTO, but he has not backed away from the border monitoring demand. Once Russia becomes a member, Georgia can sue Russia in the organization's courts for banning imports of Georgian vegetables, wine and mineral water, so long a source of disagreement between the two sides.

Russia is expected before the end of 2011 to join the World Trade Organization. "I believe this may be achieved. We hope this can be achieved. Overall, there have not been many resolved problems."

## Notes

accession：加入，到达
subsidy：津贴，补助金
separatist：独立主义(者)的；分离主义(者)的
consensus：(意见等)一致，一致同意
leverage：力量，影响
allegation：指控

# 普京敦促尽快做出决定接纳俄罗斯加入世贸组织

俄罗斯总理弗拉基米尔·普京在宣布明年参加竞选总统之后首次对

投资者公开讲话并说道,俄罗斯的主要贸易伙伴应该尽快做出决定,是否接纳俄罗斯加入世贸组织。

俄罗斯申请加入世贸组织迄今为止已有 18 年的时间。本周,美俄双方的官员都表示,俄罗斯作为当今世贸组织外的最大经济体距离组织成员身份仅一步之遥。

谈到目前俄入世的障碍,普京说,总体而言,俄方已与欧美国家就俄汽车工业组装和农业补贴等问题基本达成共识,但与格鲁吉亚关系问题悬而未决。

现存的唯一障碍是,世贸组织成员国格鲁吉亚要求在俄罗斯与两个分离主义地区阿布哈兹、南奥塞梯之间的海关通关点设立国际监督。俄罗斯强势控制着这两个地区,却在官方上称其为独立的国家。俄罗斯拒绝国际监督。

接纳新成员入世通常要得到现有成员的一致同意。在现有的 153 个世贸成员当中,格鲁吉亚特别反对俄罗斯的加入。

俄罗斯从 1993 就开始申请加入世贸组织,当时"世贸"名为关税与贸易总协定。但一系列的争端一而再再而三地阻挠俄罗斯的入世进程,包括航空税和鸡肉国际贸易的争议,还有对俄罗斯纵容侵犯知识产权的指控。俄罗斯的入世谈判员似乎已经扫清了俄入世的绝大多数障碍。诸如肉类进口、卫生标准和激励俄方汽车生产上的分歧在这周内都得到了解决。世界银行表示,俄罗斯入世不但有益于本国经济,向俄罗斯出口的公司也会从中获利。

普京在莫斯科出席由国有银行俄罗斯外贸银行主办的第三届"俄罗斯在召唤"投资论坛时表示,关于俄罗斯是否需要入世的问题在俄商界尚有争议,"俄罗斯入世对俄有利有弊。但总体而言,利大于弊。俄罗斯不会放弃入世目标,但前提是俄罗斯没有被提出无法接受的条件。"

普京在投资论坛上说,"我有一个问题。"

"我们在欧美的主要贸易伙伴到底想不想要俄罗斯加入世贸组织?"他问道,"没有必要拿格鲁吉亚的问题当挡箭牌。如果他们愿意,他们就可以加快俄入世的脚步,尤其是考虑到我们已经在大多数问题上做出了让步。"

普京在演讲中指出他不希望看到全球经济跌入第二轮的衰退,因为俄罗斯作为石油出口国或多或少地会受到牵连。

另外,普京早些时候接受记者采访时说,尽管欧元区一些国家面临主权债务危机,但他对欧元有信心。普京还说,"俄罗斯与欧洲建立亲善关系是一种必然。"

明显是为了安抚有意在俄罗斯投资的金融团体,普京在讲话中说道,广受赞誉的前俄罗斯财政部长库德林(上个月离职)仍然是"我们团队中的一员"。他还说,虽然他可能没有确定的职位,但"我们会一起工作"。

俄罗斯第一副总理舒瓦洛夫在访问华盛顿之后于星期二透露,美国朋友正在为我们入世积极游说其他成员国。他们一天24小时工作,忙着说服其他世贸成员国接受俄罗斯的申请。走过将近20年的历程我们已经非常接近目标了。他说。

普京说,美国和欧洲国家曾经要求俄罗斯和格鲁吉亚谈判解决争议。但是,俄格双方从3月开始谈判以来没有取得任何进展。

普京上个月底宣布竞选下一任总统使得现在的贸易谈判显得更加重要,谈判也能体现国际社会对普京参选的反应。普京的言语表示,他希望美国和欧洲国家给格鲁吉亚施压使其同意俄罗斯入世。

格鲁吉亚总统说,俄罗斯入世对格鲁吉亚有利,但是他不会在要求边境监督问题上退让。一旦俄罗斯入世,格鲁吉亚就可以在世贸组织的法庭上控诉俄罗斯禁止进口格鲁吉亚蔬菜、红酒和矿泉水,这是两国长久以来争端的根源之一。

俄罗斯希望在2011年底前加入世贸组织。"我相信这可能实现。我们希望这能够实现。整体而言,已经不存在尚未解决的难题了。"

**More to Read**

　　加入世贸组织的基本条件就是"市场经济体制"。而俄罗斯，受到前苏联体制影响，世界上大部分国家是不承认俄罗斯拥有完全"市场经济体制"的国家，此为一（中国也曾经面对这样的问题）。关税不够自由化，由于俄罗斯对内的农业保护政策以及轻工业保护政策，相关税收一直很高，外加俄罗斯海关贪污腐化严重，海关税收一直很混乱，所以难以拿出稳定而有效的关税策略，难以得到其他世贸成员国信任，此为二。俄罗斯入世已经成为一些国家牵制俄罗斯的政治工具，此为三。综上所述，可以看到俄罗斯的入世之旅必然是艰难复杂的。

## Reading Guidance

纵观过去的30多年，中国吸收外资，大力发展出口导向的制造业，成为"世界工厂"。长期以来，"廉价"是中国制造的代名词，然而近年来随着人民币升值、劳动力成本上涨和通胀压力的加大，中国原有廉价劳动力优势渐失。很多企业开始把生产工厂转移到劳动力成本更廉价的东南亚国家。从2010年开始，"产自越南"的字样越来越多地出现在了中国耐克鞋专柜上。耐克运动鞋都是外包生产的。2010年以前，中国是其最大的生产国，但从2010年起，越南"上位"，取代了中国的"老大"位置。近期，很多学者和官员开始反思中国经济的发展模式，认为中国单纯依赖廉价劳动力的低成本模式正在面临越来越大的挑战。随着世界经济一体化的不断深入，中国作为"世界工厂"的角色需要做些什么样的调整呢？

# Higher Production Costs Shift Chinese Manufacturing

For decades, China's factories have supplied the world with cheap goods—from denim jeans to desktop computers. But export prices are expected to go up as Chinese manufacturers are hit largely by higher wages, more expensive raw materials and an appreciating currency.

观 察 OBSERVATION

During her recent visit to Beijing, Brazil's President Dilma Rousseff said Foxconn International Holdings, the company that manufactures Apple's popular iPhone, plans to spend $12 billion building factories in her country.

For some time, Foxconn has been expanding outside of its traditional manufacturing base in southern China, shifting north to Hebei province, to cut costs. The company, which employs hundreds of thousands of workers in China, reported a loss for 2010 because of higher production costs.

Companies increasingly are moving out of southern China's manufacturing center in the Pearl River Delta as profits decline.

Stanley Lau is managing director of Renley Watch Manufacturing Company. He also heads the Pearl River Delta Council of the Hong Kong Federation of Industries.

"Wages are going up. The minimum wage has gone up by about 20 percent in 2010. And again this year wages have gone up by 20 percent roughly," said Lau. "When you look at any part of the world, I think you cannot find any other place with such kind of increase in wages."

What is more, he says, the cost of raw materials such as cotton, plastics and electronic components, is rising. Although the Chinese currency has been rising against the dollar, which could help ease rising costs for imported raw materials, manufacturers say even locally made materials are getting more expensive. China's inflation rate reached 5.4 percent in March, the highest in nearly three years.

At the same time, the Yuan's appreciation, which the United States and other Western nations say is essential to reduce China's trade imbalance, makes Chinese products more expensive overseas.

Li and Fung, a Hong Kong sourcing company that supplies the U.S. retailer Wal-mart and other global retail chains, says Chinese export prices will increase as much as 15 percent this year. Company executives last month warned that Chinese goods are entering a new era of rising prices.

The challenges Chinese exporters confront are not new. They have been struggling for a breakthrough over the past two years. In 2008, China put a new law into effect, which increased factory workers' salaries. At that time, manufacturers warned that many of them would be forced to close because of rising wages.

Pansy Yau, deputy chief economist of the Hong Kong Trade Development Council, says Chinese exports have stayed strong since then.

"When we look at the share of China export in Europe and the United States, we find that the import share from China continues to increase. It proves that China is not only competing on cost because after all these years the wages in China are already higher than some Southeast Asian countries and other low-cost countries." Said Yau.

The Chinese government has been encouraging manufacturers to move factories to poorer inland regions as a way to distribute economic development. Lau says not all industries can do so because they rely on the efficient supply chain in southern China, near other factories making needed components.

Southern China is blessed with deep ports that allow access for container ships bringing raw materials and carrying finished products to the rest of the world. Also, electricity and water supply are stable. Moving factories inland could prove costlier than staying put because companies may have to pay more in shipping costs.

When it comes to moving overseas, the Federation of Industries' Lau says it will be easiest for textile manufacturers to relocate to places like Vietnam and Indonesia, because the infrastructure is already there.

"Years ago when they had a problem with the export quotas, many textile industries moved part of their production to these countries in order to get a better quota for their textile products," said Lau. "So there's a good set up in those countries. For the other industries like electronics, plastics, the watch and clock industries, it's more difficult because if you're going to move you need the whole supply chain to move together with you. You will have problems in the delivery of parts."

At the Hong Kong Trade Development Council, economist Yau says the difficulty that Chinese exporters are feeling could well reverberate in supermarkets and shops across the world. She says it is inevitable that rising costs will be passed on to customers.

"Once they can prove that their product is good and has value for money, then they have the bargaining power to ask for a price increase," added Yau.

China's ruling Communist Party has made clear it wants to hold the line on prices—for goods sold at home and abroad. The government is working to press down inflation to make sure high prices for food and housing do not spark unrest. And Beijing has moved slowly on its pledge to let the Yuan trade more freely fearing that a sharp gain in the exchange rate could make exports even more expensive, forcing factories to close and eliminate jobs.

## Notes

Foxconn International Holdings：富士康国际控股有限公司
Renley Watch Manufacturing Company：运年表业有限公司
appreciation：增值；感激；欣赏
imbalance：不平衡；不均衡
stay put：留在原地
infrastructure：结构，基础设施
reverberate：回响，反响，反射

# 成本升高迫使中国厂商撤离沿海省份

中国的工厂在过去几十年来向世界提供廉价商品,种类从牛仔裤到台式电脑无所不包。但是随着工薪上涨、原料价格升高和人民币升值,中国产品的出口价格预计也会水涨船高。出口商目前正计划将工厂从沿海省份迁往内陆地区,或者海外,以迎接这些挑战。

巴西总统罗塞芙近期在北京表示,富士康公司计划投资120亿美元,在巴西建造工厂。富士康是苹果电脑公司热门产品 iPhone 的制造商。

富士康过去一段时间以来一直都在努力将传统生产基地从中国南方迁到北方的河北省,以降低价格。这家公司在中国有雇员数十万,由于生产成本上涨,2010年出现亏损。

利润下滑导致很多企业都将工厂从中国南方珠三角地区的传统制造基地迁出。

刘展灏是香港工业总会珠三角工业协会会长、运年表业有限公司董事长。

他说:"工资在上涨。2010年,最低工资上调了20%。今年,工资再次上涨了大约20%。在世界上其他地方,我们看不到工资如此迅速地上涨。"

刘展灏还说,棉花、塑料、电子零部件等原材料的成本也在上涨。尽管中国人民币的升值可以在一定程度上抵消进口原材料涨价,但是制造商们抱怨说,本地产的原材料正在变得更加昂贵。今年3月,中国通胀率达到5.4%,这是3年来的最高水平。

与此同时,人民币升值使得中国的出口产品变得更加昂贵。美国和其他西方国家认为,人民币升值对于减少中国贸易失衡至关重要。

香港供货商利丰有限公司向沃尔玛和一些其他主要全球零售商供货。该公司认为,今年中国出口商品价格将上涨15%。该公司总裁上个月警告说,中国商品正在进入涨价的新阶段。

中国出口商面临的挑战并不是新的。他们在过去两年一直寻求突破。2008年,中国实施了一项新法律,增加工厂工人的工资。当时,很多制造商就警告说,不断上涨的工资会把我们逼上绝路,关门歇业。

香港贸发局副总经济师邱丽萍说,中国出口仍然强劲。

她说:"我们看一下中国出口在美国和欧洲市场的表现,就会发现中国的市场份额仍然在扩大。这说明,中国的出口优势不仅仅局限于成本方面。经过过去几年的变化,中国的工资水平事实上已经高于一些东南亚国家和其他低成本国家。"

中国政府鼓励制造商把工厂转移到相对贫穷的内陆地区,以此促进经济发展平衡。邱丽萍说,并非所有行业都可以完成这种转移,因为很多企业依赖华南地区的供应链,离不开生产所需零部件的工厂。

华南地区深水港密集,集装箱货轮可以在此装卸进口的原材料和出口到世界各地的制成品。另外,这里水电供应稳定。将工厂迁入内地将增加运输成本,对于企业来说可能得不偿失。

至于将生产线迁往海外,香港工业总会珠三角工业协会会长刘展灏说,纺织业制造商转移到越南和印度尼西亚等国可能最容易,因为这些地方已经有现成的基础设施。

刘展灏说:"几年前,当这些企业面临出口配额问题时,它们已经把一些生产线转移到这些国家,以便获得更好的配额。所以这些国家已经有了设备。对于电子产品、塑料、钟表等行业来说,就更困难一些。因为如果你转移生产线的话,整个供应链都要跟着转移。否则零部件的运送就会出问题。"

香港贸发局副总经济师邱丽萍说,"中国出口商遇到的困难将在全球范围内的超市和商场里产生连锁反应。"她还说,"生产成本的提高将不可避免地转嫁给消费者。"

邱丽萍总结说:"当企业可以证明他们的产品质量优秀,物有所值,它

们就可以在定价方面掌握主动权。"

中国政府明确表示,要控制国内物价和出口产品价格上涨过快。中国政府正在试图抑制通胀,并确保粮价和房价上涨不至于造成社会动荡。同时,中国在人民币升值问题上格外谨慎,以防过快升值造成出口产品过于昂贵,导致工厂关门和就业机会丧失。

**More to Read**

在金融危机条件下,中国的经济产业转型已经成为了一个重要话题。国际上,美国等西方国家一直指责中国操纵汇率,因而对于人民币的打压势头一浪高过一浪。在国内,更多劳动者期待提高工资水平,改善经济环境。因此,有学者提出趁此机会进行经济产业升级,并将经济发展模式由出口导向转变为消费拉动,以此应对外部挑战和内部需求。然而,经济模式转型是一项艰巨的任务。经济转型本身也可能带来诸如失业率上升等一系列社会问题。如何在保持国内生产总值增长和社会稳定的同时转换发展轨道,这不仅事关中国今后30年的经济发展进程,更关乎中国是否能够顺利崛起。

观察 OBSERVATION

**Reading Guidance**

　　2001年的阿富汗战争是以美国为首的联军对阿富汗基地组织和塔利班的一场战争，是美国对"9·11事件"的报复，同时也标志着反恐战争的开始。联军官方指这场战争的目的是逮捕本·拉登等基地组织成员并惩罚塔利班对恐怖分子的支援。而本·拉登已于2011年5月1日被美军击毙。

　　阿富汗战争爆发10周年之际，联合国的一份调查报告称，今年以来，阿富汗国内安全局势明显恶化。阿富汗总统卡尔扎伊说，阿富汗政府及其国际伙伴仍然不能向阿富汗人民提供安全保障。阿富汗人对他们的未来感到失望和不确定。

　　10月7日，数以千计的阿富汗人为纪念阿富汗战争10周年在首都喀布尔街头举行示威，要求国际部队立即从阿富汗撤军。阿富汗民众对进驻阿富汗的外国军队的看法，近年来也越来越多的转向负面，他们认为外国军队进入阿富汗是对其领土的侵略。示威者在喀布尔街头集会，他们手举谴责外国军队进入阿富汗的标语，并把阿富汗平民的死亡归咎于美国及其盟国。在游行示威中，一些抗议者点燃了美国国旗。

# Afghanistan 10 Years Later

The U. S. and other NATO forces on October 7, 2001 attacked al-Qaida

extremists and their Taliban allies in Afghanistan, less than a month after the September 11 terrorist attacks. That military operation drove the Taliban from power. But the conflict that began so promisingly 10 years ago is still going on—the longest war in U. S. history.

Few expected the Taliban government in Afghanistan to fall as quickly as it did 10 years ago. But equally surprising, NATO forces are still fighting Taliban and al-Qaida insurgents 10 years later. It was in late 2001 that Afghan forces, aided by a U. S. bombing campaign, drove the Taliban from Kabul. But then Taliban and al-Qaida leaders fled into the mountains of Tora Bora, escaped into Pakistan and the fighting has raged ever since.

"There were a number of mistakes that were made over the years, and definitely in the years before 2009," said General Carsten Jacobson, ISAF spokesman. "I would say the first one was to underestimate the Taliban because we were blinded by the success that we had in 2001 and 2002. We didn't bring enough forces into the country."

Without enough allied troops to stop them, Taliban fighters began slipping back into Afghanistan and regaining territory. NATO forces could do little but hold on. In 2003, the U. S. also switched its attention to a new war in Iraq.

"Lessons were drawn out of Iraq," said General Jacobson. "The right lessons were drawn out of Iraq and basically it was becoming very clear by the end of 2008 and through 2009 that something had to be done to defeat the insurgency and in parallel to build up security forces."

In addition, U. S. President Barack Obama shifted attention back to Afghanistan. More troops arrived in 2009.

And the build up of Afghan security forces also increased, coupled with an aggressive program using unmanned drove planes to strike at insurgent havens in Pakistan's border region. In a visit to Afghanistan before stepping down as chairman of the U. S. Joint Chiefs of Staff, Admiral Mike Mullen had this to say.

观察 OBSERVATION

"The enemies of Afghanistan and those who seek nothing more than to strike out against our coalition have been dealt heavy blows over the last year," he said. "They've been pushed out of sanctuary. They've been denied influence over local populations. They've been hunted. Their leaders killed or captured by the score."

President Obama says there is enough progress in Afghanistan to remove about one-third of American troops by September of next year.

The plan will bring home all of the extra troops he ordered sent to Afghanistan eighteen months ago. And Mr. Obama says American troops will continue coming home as Afghan security forces move into the lead.

He calls this a transition process in a mission that will change from combat to support. This process will be complete by 2014, he says, and the Afghan people will be responsible for their own security. Mr. Obama said peace in Afghanistan will require a political settlement which could include the Taliban.

Several NATO nations with troops in Afghanistan plan to end their combat role there by 2014. Until then, the fighting continues and Afghanistan remains a nation at war.

Afghans are expressing a mixture of disappointment and uncertainty about their future, as they mark the anniversary of the start of the Afghan war.

While the Taliban were ousted from power, 10 years later, many Afghans still feel let down by the international effort to rid their country of the Taliban and normalize its institutions.

Sitfatullah Safi is the deputy chief of Afghan government media relations. "There is a lot of achievement in Afghanistan in the last ten years, but not as much as people expect," said Safi.

Safi says the biggest disappointment is the failure to ensure Afghanistan's security. "The Afghan people were hoping that international forces in the last ten years should secure their lives, and secure the Afghan borders—especially the eastern and southern borders," added Safi. "But unfortunately today, the security situation is a big concern of the Afghan government and people."

Wahidullah Ghazikhail, an independent Afghan researcher, is blunt about the U. S. -led stabilization mission. "They are not successful in this 10-year war in Afghanistan," said Ghazikhail.

Ghazikhail says many Afghans were looking to the United States and its international partners for something similar to what followed World War II. "They helped Europe, especially Germany. And they went there with the Marshall Plan. And people were expecting the rehabilitation, rebuilding the nation, democracy, and reconstruction. But unfortunately we were expecting more," added Ghazikhail.

Among ordinary Afghans, opinions about the decade-long, multi-billion dollar effort are mixed.

Ahmad Yossuf, a construction worker, has a bleak view of the state of his country. Neither the Taliban nor this government ever gave us anything, he says. It's the poor people, he says, who are the losers.

His fellow laborer, Nesar Ahmad, sees a brighter side. He says that in the past ten years, development programs have been implemented, a national army has been formed, bridges and schools have been built, and some degree of democracy has been established. So it is a fact, he says, that some positive changes have taken place.

## Notes

extremist：极端主义者,过激分子
insurgent：暴动者,叛乱分子
coalition：同盟
sanctuary：避难所
oust：驱逐,罢免
blunt：钝的;直言不讳的

观察 OBSERVATION

# 10年战后阿富汗

在2001年9月11日美国遭受恐怖袭击之后不到一个月,美军于10月7日与北约其他成员国的部队一道在阿富汗对基地组织极端分子和他们的塔利班盟友发动了进攻。那场军事行动推翻了塔利班政权。10年前开始的这场有望速战速决的战争现在仍在进行,这是美国历史上最长的一次战争。

很少有人能料到,阿富汗的塔利班政府在10年前那么迅速地垮台。可是同样令人惊奇的是,10年之后,北约部队仍在与塔利班和基地组织的叛乱分子作战。2001年年底,阿富汗部队在美国空中轰炸的援助下,把塔利班赶出喀布尔。然而,塔利班和基地组织领导人逃入托拉波拉山区,进入巴基斯坦。从那至今,战斗一直在激烈进行。

北约驻阿富汗的国际安全援助部队发言人雅各布森将军说:"过去这些年,特别是在2009年之前,我们犯过一些错误。第一个错误就是低估了塔利班,因为那时在2001年和2002年所取得的胜利冲昏了我们的头脑。我们没有调动足够的部队去阿富汗。"

因为没有足够的联军部队阻止他们,塔利班的战斗人员开始悄悄地返回阿富汗,重新占领了一些地盘。对此,北约部队几乎无能为力,只有坚持。2003年,美国也把注意力转向了伊拉克的新战争。

雅各布森将军说:"我们从伊拉克战争中获得了有益的经验。在2008年年底至2009年期间,我们基本上已经十分清楚,必须采取某些行动以击败叛乱分子,与此同时,还要加强我们的安全部队。"

此外,奥巴马总统把注意力再次转向阿富汗。2009年,更多的美军被

派往阿富汗。

阿富汗的安全部队也得到加强,同时也实行了一项很有力度的计划,使用无人驾驶飞机向巴基斯坦边境地区叛乱分子的藏身处发动空袭。美军参谋长联席会议主席迈克·马伦海军上将在离任前出访阿富汗期间说了这样一番话。

马伦上将说:"阿富汗的敌人以及那些只想袭击我们联军的人去年遭到重创。他们被赶出藏身处,已无法对当地人施加影响。他们受到了追捕。他们大批的头目不是被打死就是被抓获。"

奥巴马总统表示在阿富汗已经取得了足够进展,可以在明年9月前撤出三分之一的美国部队。

这项撤军计划将撤回18个月前奥巴马下令派往阿富汗的所有增兵部队。奥巴马表示,随着阿富汗安全部队逐步成为主导力量,美国部队将继续撤离回国。

奥巴马表示,这是由作战任务转为支持任务的阶段性过渡过程。这个过程将于2014年前完成,届时阿富汗人民将对自己的安全负责。奥巴马表示,阿富汗的和平将需要一个包括塔利班在内的政治解决方案。

向阿富汗出兵的几个北约成员国计划在2014年以前结束他们的战斗任务。而在此之前,战斗仍在继续,阿富汗仍然是一个处于战争状态的国家。

在阿富汗战争10周年之际,阿富汗人对他们的未来感到失望和不确定。

虽然塔利班已被赶下台,但10年后的今天,许多阿富汗人依然对消除塔利班和恢复社会秩序的国际努力感到失望。

阿富汗政府的媒体关系事务副主管西特法图拉·萨菲说:"过去10年阿富汗取得了许多成就,但是没有人们所期望的那样多。"

萨菲说,最大的失望在于没能确保阿富汗的安全。他说:"阿富汗人民希望在过去10年国际部队应该能确保他们的人身安全,维护阿富汗的边界安全,尤其是东部和南部边界。但不幸的是,今天,安全局势是阿富汗政府和人民的一大担忧。"

瓦西杜拉·加齐克黑尔是阿富汗的一名独立研究人员,他直言不讳地评价美国领导的维持稳定任务说:"他们在阿富汗的这场10年战争中没有获得成功。"

加齐克黑尔说,许多阿富汗人指望美国及其国际伙伴推行类似于第二次世界大战后的做法。他说:"他们(在二战后)帮助欧洲,尤其是德国。他们在欧洲推行马歇尔计划。人们期待复兴、国家重建和民主。但不幸的是,我们期望的更多。"

阿富汗普通民众对于这场长达10年、耗资数十亿的努力有着不同看法。

建筑工人阿迈德·约瑟夫对阿富汗的状况感到沮丧。他说:"不论是塔利班还是这个政府,都没有给我们带来任何东西。他说,输家是可怜的民众。"

他的同事内萨·阿迈德则看到较为光明的一面。他说,过去10年来,实施了发展项目,建立了国家军队,兴建了桥梁和学校,还建立了某种程度上的民主。他说,事实上已经发生了一些积极的改变。

**More to Read**

当年美军大军压境,动作神速地把塔利班赶出了喀布尔。美国人一时间似乎忘记了曾经的老对手——苏联在阿富汗的遭遇。历史是如此的吊诡,世界上拥有最强大军队的两个国家都在阿富汗这块不毛之地陷入泥沼。阿富汗的安全形势目前仍然不容乐观,暗杀、恐怖袭击总是充斥着有关阿富汗的新闻报道。卡尔扎伊领导的阿富汗政府承受着内外重重压力,而这个政府本身的团结、效率和廉洁都存在严重问题。美军撤出后,阿富汗是否会向当年苏军撤走以后又陷入内战?这是包括美国人在内的很多人担心的问题。可是不撤,美国的选民们才不会答应呢!要知道,奥巴马就是打着"撤军"旗号上台的。所以,当美国总统可真不容易,尤其再赶上前任是个冒失、好战、不知如何审慎使用权力的"牛仔总统",你就有的好瞧了。

## Reading Guidance

朝核问题始于20世纪90年代初。当时，美国根据卫星资料怀疑朝鲜开发核武器，扬言要对朝鲜的核设施实行检查。朝鲜则宣布无意也无力开发核武器，同时指责美国在韩国部署核武器威胁了它的安全。第一次朝鲜半岛核危机由此爆发。朝核问题自2002年10月再次凸显以来，为了朝核问题的和平解决，中国政府曾多方进行斡旋，最终促成朝鲜、美国、中国、韩国、俄罗斯、日本六国同意就政治解决朝核问题举行会谈。在中国及有关各方的努力下，从2003年8月开始至今，六方会谈已进行到第六轮。2009年4月，朝鲜外务省在平壤发表声明，宣布退出朝核问题六方会谈，并将按原状恢复已去功能化的核设施。

2011年7月28日，朝鲜与美国在纽约重启为期两天的双边对话，国际社会密切关注。这是自2009年以来朝美首次展开对话，也是朝鲜高官罕有地受美方邀请访问美国。

# U. S. And North Korea Meet on Nuclear Issue

The United States on Thursday characterized its first day of exploratory talks with North Korea as "serious and business-like." The two days of meetings are aimed at determining whether Pyongyang is willing to resume negotiations over its nuclear program. The talks are the highest-level meeting between the two countries since a visit to North Korea by a senior U. S. envoy nearly two years ago.

U. S. Special Envoy for North Korea Stephen Bosworth led the U. S. interagency delegation that met with North Korean Vice Foreign Minister Kim Kae-Gwan at the United States Mission to the United Nations.

The diplomats met most of Thursday and for a little over three hours on Friday. Afterwards, Ambassador Bosworth told reporters the talks were designed to explore the willingness of North Korea to take concrete and irreversible steps toward denuclearization.

"In that regard, these were constructive and business-like discussions," said Bosworth. He went on to say that the resumption of the Six-Party talks begun in 2003, but which North Korea withdrew from in 2009, is possible.

North Korea pulled out of the Six-Party Talks in April 2009 after the U. N. Security Council condemned Pyongyang's launch of a long-range rocket, in violation of a council resolution.

"We reiterated that the path is open to North Korea towards the resumption of talks, improved relations with the United States, and greater regional stability, if North Korea demonstrates through its actions that it supports the resumption of the Six-Party process as a committed and constructive partner," he said.

Ambassador Bosworth said that before deciding on next steps to resume the process, the United States would consult closely with South Korea and its other partners in the Six-Party talks. Those countries include China, Japan and Russia.

U. S. Special Envoy for North Korea Stephen Bosworth greeted the head of the North Korean delegation, Vice Foreign Minister Kim Kae-gwan, with a handshake when he arrived in the morning. Then they disappeared into the concrete tower until Mr. Kim emerged at midday for a lunch break.

The North Korean official traveled by car the short distance around the cor-

ner to his hotel, perhaps to avoid the throng of mostly Asian reporters and cameramen waiting for him outside the U.S. Mission. But he was unsuccessful. At his hotel, more reporters awaited him.

Kim stopped briefly to respond to their questions about the talks, saying, "The atmosphere was good" and that the meeting was "constructive and interesting." with an exchange of views on general issues.

At the State Department in Washington, Deputy Spokesman Mark Toner said the United States will use the talks, which it characterizes as "exploratory", to determine whether North Korea is serious about fulfilling its nuclear obligations, including ending its nuclear program.

"There was the meeting in Bali between North and South Korea," said Toner. "It was constructive. Now we have embarked on these exploratory discussions. We are quite clear broadly what we are looking for, which is for North Korea to live up to its commitments in the 2005 joint statement as well as its international obligations. And it needs to take concrete steps toward denuclearization."

In exchange for North Korea meeting its obligations, the United States, China, South Korea, Japan and Russia—all members of the Six-Party Talks—would offer Pyongyang food and energy assistance as well as diplomatic incentives.

Pyongyang wants full six-party talks to resume. But South Korea says the North must first clearly indicate it intends to abandon its nuclear program. South Korean Foreign Minister Kim Sung-hwan said Pyongyang must abide by previous promises to denuclearize before any new round of six-party talks can resume. "Seoul and Washington will keep urging North Korea to demonstrate through specific actions that it has true intentions to abandon its nuclear programs."

China has been pushing for their quick resumption. But the U.S., South Korea and Japan have been more cautious, saying North Korea must first implement actions it agreed to take in previous negotiations.

North Korean leader Kim Jong Ⅱ told Russia's Itar-Tass news agency last week six-way talks should resume without preconditions. He also reaffirmed his commitment six years ago to gradually reduce North Korea's nuclear programs in exchange for massive aid, enhanced diplomatic relations and security guarantees.

## Notes

irreversible：不可逆转的，不可挽回的
condemn：谴责；宣告……有罪
reiterate：重申
throng：一大群，大量
reaffirm：重申

# 美朝核会谈

美国和朝鲜在星期四进行的第一天试探性会谈被形容为"严肃认真而且就事论事"。这次为期两天的会谈目的，是确定朝鲜是否愿意就其核计划恢复谈判。这是自美国一名高级特使将近两年前访问朝鲜以来，两国之间最高层级的会谈。

美国朝鲜问题特使斯蒂芬·博斯沃思率领了一个美国跨部门小组在美国常驻联合国代表团驻地会见了朝鲜外务省第一副相金桂冠。

这些外交官的会晤主要是在7月28日（星期四）进行的，星期五的会

晤只持续了三个多小时。会晤之后，博斯沃思特使告诉记者说，会谈的目的是为了试探朝鲜在无核化问题上采取切实与不可逆转的步骤的意愿。

博斯沃思说："从这方面来看，这次会谈是具有建设性和讲求实际的。"他接着说，六方会谈于2003年开始，但朝鲜于2009年从会谈中退出。恢复六方会谈是可能的。

朝鲜于2009年4月退出六方会谈。在此之前，联合国安理会谴责平壤试射远程导弹违反了安理会的决议。

博斯沃思说："我们重申，如果朝鲜通过行动表现出它作为一个坚定和积极的伙伴支持恢复六方会谈进程，那么，对朝鲜来说，恢复六方会谈、改善与美国的关系以及实现更大程度的地区稳定的道路就是敞开的。"

博斯沃思特使说，在为恢复六方会谈进程采取下一步措施前，美国将与韩国以及六方会谈其他各方密切磋商。那些国家包括中国、日本和俄罗斯。

当朝鲜副外长金桂冠在早上抵达会场时，还和美国的朝鲜问题特使博斯沃茨握手致意。接着他们就走进不对外开放的会场，直到午餐时候，金桂冠才再度现身。

也许是为了避开守候在美国代表团门外的大部分亚洲记者和摄影人员，这位朝鲜官员乘车返回他近在咫尺的旅馆。但是他没有成功。因为有更多的记者在他下榻的旅馆等候。

金桂冠短暂止步，回答在场记者们有关这次会谈的提问。他说，会谈的气氛良好，而且这次会谈有趣且具有建设性，双方还就一般议题交换了观点。

在华盛顿，美国国务院副发言人特纳表示，美国仍然将利用这次试探性的会谈，来确定朝鲜是否认真地履行其包括停止核计划在内的核义务。

特纳说："在印度尼西亚的巴厘，美国和朝鲜举行过会谈。那次会谈具有建设性。现在我们开始了这些实验性的讨论。我们非常明了我们追求的是什么。对于2005年的共同声明以及其国际义务的承诺，朝鲜应该怎么做。而且需要采取切实步骤来迈向无核化。"

为了换取朝鲜履行其义务，所有六方会谈的成员国——美国、中国、韩

观察 OBSERVATION

国、日本和俄罗斯,都将为平壤提供粮食和紧急援助以及外交奖励。

朝鲜目前希望恢复六方会谈,但是韩国方面表示,朝鲜必须首先明确表明将放弃其核武器项目。韩国外交通商部长官金星焕说,在新一轮六方会谈之前,平壤必须首先信守以前放弃核武器项目的承诺。他说,"首尔和华盛顿将继续敦促朝鲜通过具体的行动来表明他们是要真正放弃核武器项目。"

中国一直主张尽快恢复谈判。但是,美国、韩国和日本则更加谨慎。他们指出,朝鲜必须首先把在以前谈判中的承诺落实为实际行动。

朝鲜领导人金正日上星期在接受俄罗斯塔斯社采访时说,六方会谈应在不设先决条件的情况下重新启动。他还重申,他将履行6年前的承诺,逐步减少朝鲜的核计划,以此换取大量的援助,加强外交关系和安全保障。

**More to Read**

朝核问题自1994年爆发以来,国际社会始终没有放弃实现半岛无核化的努力。对朝鲜来说,核计划是与建立"强盛大国"策略联系在一起的。但更重要的是,朝鲜已经将核问题作为与西方大国,尤其是美国进行直接接触和谈判的重要筹码。对美国而言,朝核的存在是对其东北亚乃至整个远东政策的挑战,必须加以彻底的解决。作为地区大国的中国原本极力促成了有关六方在北京通过"六方会谈"的形式处理朝核问题。但由于各方立场始终无法协调统一,当前会谈处于停滞的状态。但从另一个角度来看,朝鲜和美国的实力差距实在太大,通过双边谈判的方式并不利于朝鲜。回归多边会谈可能仍然是朝鲜的最终选择。因此,朝美在日内瓦的接触有可能预示着出现了重启六方会谈的希望。

## Reading Guidance

2011年7月8日,联合国人权高级专员皮莱在墨西哥城举行记者会,总结此次为期五天的墨西哥访问。她赞扬了墨西哥在推动人权发展方面取得的一些成就,但对该国不断升级的严重暴力罪行表达了关注。皮莱对于在打击有组织犯罪过程中不断出现的有关政府人员过度使用武力和侵犯人权的状况表示担忧。

自2006年年底以来,缉毒成为墨西哥政府的首要任务。在墨西哥,几乎每天都会出现与毒品有关的新闻。鉴于墨西哥反毒战的艰辛,美国《时代》周刊将墨西哥政府打击贩毒评选为2010年的"十大新闻"之一。缉毒行动也让墨政府付出了沉重代价。涉毒暴力加剧造成社会治安形势恶化。据估计,暴力犯罪给墨西哥造成的经济损失占其国内生产总值的15%以上。

# Drug War in Mexico Raises Human Rights Concerns

The U. N. High Commissioner for Human Rights, Navi Pillay, is concluding a weeklong visit to Mexico, where she expressed concern over abuse of citizens by police and soldiers fighting organized crime groups. The major effort against drug cartels and other criminal organizations that began shortly after Mexican President Felipe Calderon took office in December, 2006, has now claimed around 40 000 lives. Experts say ending official corruption and impunity is the biggest challenge the government faces in trying to win the war.

On her visit to Mexico, U. N. High Commissioner for Human Rights Navi Pillay looked into problems including abuse of migrants and women. In a meeting with President Calderon, Pillay mentioned allegations against police and military forces in the war on drug traffickers.

"I view with concern the increasing reports of human rights violations attributed to state agents in the fight against organized crime," Pillay said.

She said authorities should not view respect for human rights as an obstacle, but as part of the solution in combating crime.

President Calderon responded that the worst abusers of human rights in Mexico are the criminal gangs that have tortured, violently damaged and killed thousands of people. The drug cartels are fighting the government and each other as they compete for lucrative smuggling routes and drug profits.

At the inauguration of a new criminal investigation laboratory, supported in part by funds from the United States, President Calderon spoke of the need for reform and modernization of police forces.

Calderon said human rights are protected when police use evidence to prove their case rather than confessions that might be made under duress.

Human rights groups complain that, in far too many cases, police without proper investigative skills detain suspects and torture them until they confess.

But President Calderon also condemned faults in the system that have allowed criminals to escape justice.

Calderon added that as long as criminals get away with crimes and go unpunished they will continue their illegal operations. He said Mexico must break the vicious cycle of impunity that allows transnational criminal organizations to operate.

To avoid corrupt police, Calderon has used military forces against the powerful drug cartels. But drawing on soldiers while trying to protect human rights is problematic, according to Mexico expert George Grayson of the College of

William and Mary.

"Mexico has never, never had an honest, reliable, professional police force and this goes back to colonial times," Grayson noted. "So Calderon had no choice, when he found areas of the country dominated by cartels, but to use the military and the military is trained to pursue, to capture, to kill and, in the process, there is often additional damage of civilians."

There have been many complaints from human rights activists about military abuses, but many citizens in violence-ruined areas often see soldiers as their only defense against the well-armed criminal gangs.

Citizen attitudes about police in Mexico may be part of the problem. Surveys have shown that Mexicans have little respect for their police and that paying small bribes to avoid such inconveniences as a traffic ticket is still common practice in much of the country. Mexican police are usually paid little and given only minimal training.

For the government to tackle such problems it will need public support in both spiritual and material terms. George Grayson says Mexicans in the upper and middle classes, who have been absent from this effort, need to do more and pay more.

"The elite pay little in taxes, about 10 percent of gross domestic product," Grayson added. "To give you an idea, Brazil pays 33 percent of gross domestic product in terms of taxes. Without more taxes you cannot have job creation programs, you cannot engage in regional development, you cannot restructure the public school system, you cannot improve health delivery services and, as a result, 40 percent of Mexicans live in poverty."

Part of the reason wealthy Mexicans pay so little in taxes is the government's reliance on revenues from the state-owned oil sector, which cover about a third of the federal budget. But Mexico's oil reserves are in decline and President Calderon has had limited success in opening the sector to foreign investment. So that issue, like the drug war and the effort to prevent human rights abuses, will await the person who succeeds Calderon after next year's presidential election.

## Notes

cartel：卡特尔,联合企业,垄断集团
impunity：免除惩罚
smuggle：走私,非法私运
inauguration：开幕仪式；就职典礼
vicious：恶毒的,凶残的
revenue：收入；税收

# 墨西哥打击贩毒引发人权担忧

联合国人权事务高级专员纳维·皮莱即将结束对墨西哥为期一周的访问,她对该国警察和军人在打击有组织的犯罪集团过程中践踏人权的状况表示忧虑。墨西哥总统卡尔德龙2006年12月就任后不久就展开了打击贩毒集团和其他犯罪组织的行动,这一行动目前已造成约4万人死亡。专家表示杜绝官方腐败和有罪不罚现象是墨西哥政府在缉毒战中面临的最大挑战。

在访问墨西哥期间,联合国人权事务高级专员纳维·皮莱调查了践踏移民和妇女之权利的问题。在与墨西哥总统卡尔德龙会晤时,皮莱提到了警察和军人在缉毒行动中受到的指控。

她说:"我看到越来越多的报道说,在打击有组织犯罪的战斗中国家安全人员存在违反人权的行为,我对此感到担忧。"

皮莱表示,当局不应将尊重人权看作一种障碍,而应该把它当作打击犯罪的一种办法。

卡尔德龙总统回应说，墨西哥最恶劣的人权践踏者是那些折磨、残害和打死数以千万计民众的犯罪团伙。贩毒集团与政府做斗争，同时，贩毒集团互相之间为了争夺走私路线和毒品营利也在斗争。

在由美国部分出资兴建的一个犯罪调查实验室的启动仪式上，卡尔德龙总统谈到过改革警察部队和使其现代化的必要性。

卡尔德龙总统说，当警方用证据证明犯罪事实，而不是嫌疑人在胁迫下招供时，人权就得到了保护。

人权组织抱怨说，有太多的案例显示，警方在缺乏正确调查技能的情况下扣押和折磨犯罪嫌疑人直到他们招供。

但卡尔德龙总统也指责司法系统上的漏洞，使得犯罪分子逃脱法律的制裁。

总统还说，犯罪分子只要逃脱、未受惩罚，他们就会继续胡作非为。墨西哥必须打破有罪不罚、让跨国犯罪组织继续运作的恶性循环。

为了避免使用腐败的警察，卡尔德龙动用军事力量打击有权势的毒品集团。但是墨西哥问题专家、美国威廉与玛丽学院的教授乔治·格雷森认为，动用军人而同时要设法保护人权，是很成问题的。

格雷森教授说："墨西哥从来都没有一个诚实、可靠和专业的警察部队，这可以追溯到殖民时期。所以卡尔德龙别无选择，当他发现存在有被犯罪集团控制的地区时，只好动用军人，而军人是被训练来追踪、抓获和杀戮的，所以在执行行动的过程中，通常附带有平民死伤。"

人权活动人士有很多关于军人践踏人权的抱怨，但在充斥着暴力的地区，许多民众常常把军人作为他们抵御武装犯罪团伙的唯一力量。

墨西哥民众对警察的态度可能是问题的一部分。调查显示，墨西哥人对他们的警察几乎毫不尊重，在该国大部分地区，为了避免交通罚单等麻烦事而向警察行贿仍是很普遍的现象。墨西哥警察通常工资很低，所受训练极差。

墨西哥政府为了应对这些问题，将需要公众提供精神和物质两方面的支持。威廉与玛丽学院的乔治·格雷森教授说，墨西哥的上层社会和中产阶级一直以来对这一问题的参与不足，今后需要加强参与和投入。

格雷森教授还说:"这些精英们上交的税太少,只占国内生产总值的大约10%。给你们一个参考,巴西的税收收入占国内生产总值的33%。没有更多的税收收入,就不能开展创造就业机会项目,就不能从事地区开发,不能重建公立学校体系,不能改善医疗递送服务,结果就是,墨西哥40%的人生活贫困。"

墨西哥富人交税很少的部分原因是,政府依赖国有石油区的收入,这部分收入占联邦预算的大约三分之一。但墨西哥的石油储备在下降,卡尔德龙总统在向外国投资者开放石油地区方面的作为非常有限。所以,诸如打击贩毒和遏制践踏人权的问题都要仰仗明年总统大选之后产生的卡尔德龙的继任者了。

## More to Read

毒品问题一直困扰着像墨西哥这样的美洲国家。从内部而言,贩毒问题严重影响了其国内治安,贩毒集团的力量甚至在某些地区左右了当地的政治经济走势。而从外部来看,美国认为其境内的毒品主要源自墨西哥,墨政府承受的禁毒压力可想而知。有着类似烦恼的还有哥伦比亚等南美国家。

打击贩毒和保护人权原本并不矛盾。然而在具体实践中,由于警察等执法人员急于获取口供而滥用暴力的情况并不鲜见。这就涉及"目的是否可以证明手段正当"的古老话题了。现代文明社会的基本共识是:程序正义同实质正义同样重要(如果不是更重要的话)。每个人的基本人权都必须得到尊重,即便他是一名贩毒嫌疑人也不能否定其拥有的基本人权。禁毒仅仅使用打击的方式恐怕并不能解决问题的全部。拉美地区贩毒猖獗的重要原因之一是当地人缺乏充分的工作、生活和福利保障。铤而走险去贩毒成为了这些生活在社会底层人们的选择之一。因此,发展经济、创造机会,从而提高人们的平均生活水平是这些国家禁毒治本的重要一环。

## Reading Guidance

2011年10月16日,美国总统奥巴马出席民权领袖马丁·路德·金纪念园的揭幕仪式。据有线电视新闻网报道,纪念碑最初预定于8月28日揭幕,纪念这位民权领袖发表全世界瞩目的《我有一个梦想》讲话48周年,但因飓风和地震而推迟至今。马丁·路德·金纪念园位于华盛顿市中心潮汐湖畔,国家广场上。它的诞生历经了三位总统:克林顿立项、小布什奠基、奥巴马揭幕,历时15年完成。马丁·路德·金的雕像是由中国雕塑家雷宜锌雕刻完成的。他的设计方案从全世界52个国家2000多位雕塑家的900多个方案中脱颖而出。雷宜锌的设计由两块巨型大理石组成,寓意马丁·路德·金穿越"绝望之山"并现身于"希望之石"。设计灵感来源于《我有一个梦想》中的名句。奥巴马总统在揭幕仪式上发表了讲话,呼吁国人"团结",继续金心目中的梦想。

# Thousands Gather to Dedicate Martin Luther King Jr. Memorial

Thousands of people gathered at dawn Sunday to give the new Martin Luther King Jr. Memorial a proper dedication on the National Mall.

The 30-foot-tall statue, which forms the centerpiece of a $120 million (£73 million), four-acre memorial to Dr. King, opened to the public in August in Washington. It is the only memorial on the Mall that does not honor a president or fallen soldiers.

About 1.5 million people are estimated to have visited the statue of King and the granite walls where 14 of his quotations are carved in stone. The memorial is the first on the National Mall honoring a black leader.

The monument, situated between the Lincoln and Jefferson memorials, was 15 years in the making. Its designers could not have predicted then that the monument would be dedicated by the nation's first black president.

President Barack Obama, who was just 6 years old when King was assassinated in April 1968 in Memphis, Tennessee, saluted Dr. Martin Luther King Jr. Sunday as a man who "stirred our conscience" and made the Union "more perfect".

Obama urged Americans to harness the energy of the civil rights movement for today's challenges and to remain committed to King's philosophy of peaceful resistance. "Let us draw strength from those earlier struggles," Obama said. "Change has never been simple or without controversy."

King didn't say in the famous 1963 speech that he thought there could be a black president, but he did indicate his belief in interviews that it would happen one day.

King's older sister, Christine King Farris, said she witnessed a baby become "a great hero to humanity." She said the memorial will ensure her brother's legacy will provide a source of inspiration worldwide for generations.

"He was my little brother, and I watched him grow and develop into a man who was destined for a special kind of greatness," she said. To young people in the crowd, she said King's message is that "Great dreams can come true and America is the place where you can make it happen."

King's daughter, the Rev. Bernice King, said her family is proud to witness the memorial's dedication. "Today represents another milestone in the life of America," Bernice King said.

Martin Luther King Jr. was the leading voice of the nation's modern day civil rights movement. King rose to prominence in the 1950's and 60's as the young leader of a non-violent protest movement for racial equality. "The greatness of America is the right to protest for right," he said.

On August 28, 1963, more than a quarter of a million people converged on the nation's capital for what's now known as the "March on Washington." King's most famous speech was the highlight of the historic protest for jobs and freedom.

"I have a dream that my four little children will one day live in a nation where they will not be judged by the color of their skin but by the content of their character," King said.

King's dream for a better America began to take shape in 1964. At age 35 he became the youngest recipient of the Nobel Peace Prize. At the same time the civil rights movement succeeded in pressuring lawmakers and President Lyndon Johnson to approve (The 1964 Civil Rights Act and the 1965 Voting Rights Act) landmark legislation outlawing racial segregation in public places and discriminatory practices that prevented blacks from voting.

"I want to say to the people of America and the nations of the world we [African Americans] are on the move and no wave of racism can stop us," King stated.

Not long after these achievements, though in April 1968, King was assassinated in Memphis, Tennessee.

More than four decades after his assassination, the nation is honoring Martin Luther King and his vision of racial equality with a national memorial in Washington. The cornerstone of the memorial is the "Stone of Hope", a large granite sculpture of King with his arms crossed emerging from a stone extracted from a mountain. It was carved by Chinese artist Lei Yixin. The design was inspired by a line from the famous *I Have a Dream* speech in 1963: "Out of the mountain of despair, a stone of hope."

Vernon Roberts, a visitor from New Jersey, says the Martin Luther King memorial is unique. "It gives us African Americans a perspective other than the presidential memorials that you see in Washington, D. C. It affords us the opportunity to study, to know and actually to grow. And it's a form of encouragement to all of us," he said.

Those who helped build the Martin Luther King national memorial say it is a lasting tribute to a man of peace, whose movement fought so hard for democracy, justice and improving the lives of millions of African Americans.

## Notes

assassinate：暗杀, 行刺

harness：利用

converge：聚集, 集中

legislation：立法

segregation：隔离

discriminatory：歧视的, 差别待遇的

# 万人集会为马丁·路德·金纪念园揭幕

本周日清晨, 数万人聚集在美国国家广场为刚刚落成的马丁·路德·金纪念园正式揭幕。

作为耗资 1 亿 2 千万美元(约合 7300 万英镑), 占地 4 英亩的金博士纪念园的核心之作——高 30 英尺的马丁·路德·金雕像已于今年 8 月在

华盛顿向公众开放。这是国家广场上唯一一个不是为纪念总统或是烈士而设的纪念园。

据估计，大约有150万人已经参观了马丁·路德·金雕像和刻有14句金博士名言的花岗岩石壁。这里是国家广场上第一个为黑人领袖设立的纪念园。

这个位于林肯纪念堂和杰弗逊纪念堂之间的纪念园历时15年完成。当初的设计者一定没有想到为马丁·路德·金纪念园揭幕的竟然是美国的首位黑人总统。

金博士1968年4月在田纳西州孟菲斯市遇刺身亡时，贝拉克·奥巴马总统只有6岁。本周日，奥巴马向马丁·路德·金致敬，称其为"激发了我们的良知"，并让美国变得"更加完美"的人。

奥巴马呼吁国人拿出民权运动的力量来迎接当今的挑战，继续奉行金博士的和平抵抗原则。"让我们从那些早期抗争中汲取力量。"奥巴马说，"做出改变从来都不是简简单单、毫无争议的。"

金在其1963年的著名演讲中并没有讲到他认为可能出现一名黑人总统，但他的确在一些采访中表示他相信这一天迟早会到来。

金的姐姐克里斯汀·金·法瑞斯说，她见证了一个婴儿成为"人类的大英雄"。她说，纪念园将确保其弟弟的遗产可以在全世界激励一代又一代的人。

"他是我的小弟弟，我看着他长大成人，注定成为一个伟大的男人。"她说。对于人群中的年轻人，她说金想要传达的信息是"伟大的梦想会成真，而美国就是让你梦想成真的地方"。

马丁·路德·金的女儿贝尼斯·金说，她的家人为能见证纪念园揭幕而感到骄傲。"今天代表了美国生活中的又一个里程碑。"贝尼斯·金说道。

马丁·路德·金是这个国家现代民权运动的先锋。金于20世纪50和60年代作为一名追求种族平等的非暴力抗议运动中的青年领袖变得引人注目。"美国的伟大之处在于有权利通过抗议来争取权利。"他说道。

1963年8月28日，超过25万人聚集在美国首都，现在这一运动被称为"向华盛顿进军"。金最为著名的演讲正是这一要求工作和自由的历史性抗议活动中的华章。

"我有一个梦想,有一天我的四个小孩会生活在一个不以他们的肤色,而是以他们的品格内涵来评价他们的国家。"金说道。

金追求一个更美好的美国的梦想开始形成于1964年。在35岁时,他成为了最年轻的诺贝尔和平奖获得者。与此同时,民权运动在迫使立法者和林登·约翰逊总统批准标志性的立法上(1964年民权法和1965年投票权法)获得了成果,这些法案规定在公共场所实施种族隔离和阻止黑人投票的歧视性行为为非法。

"我想对美国和世界各国人民说,我们(非洲裔美国人)正在行动,任何种族主义的浪潮都不能阻止我们。"金讲道。

但就在取得这些成就之后不久,1968年4月,金在田纳西州孟菲斯市遇刺身亡。

在他遇刺四十多年后,这个国家用一座华盛顿的国家纪念园来向马丁·路德·金及其种族平等的观念致敬。纪念碑的基石是"希望之石",也就是把金博士雕刻成双臂交叉从山石中出现的巨大花岗岩雕塑。这座塑像由中国雕刻家雷宜锌雕刻完成。设计灵感来源于马丁·路德·金在1963年所做的著名演讲《我有一个梦想》中的一句话:"我们能从绝望之山中开采出希望之石。"

来自新泽西州的参观者弗农·罗伯茨说,马丁·路德·金纪念碑是独一无二的。"和位于华盛顿的各个总统纪念碑不同,这个纪念碑让我们非洲裔美国人展望未来。让我们有机会去学习、了解和实实在在地成长。这对于我们所有人来说是一种鼓励。"他说道。

帮助建造马丁·路德·金纪念碑的人说,这是对一个和平主义者的永久赞颂。他曾经领导运动,为了争取民主、正义和提高数以百万计的非洲裔美国人的生活而奋斗不息。

**More to Read**

　　我们现在很难想象,就在20世纪60年代,在美国仍有数以百万计的黑人无权投票参加竞选。而在此之前的10年时间里,美国两任总统艾森豪威尔和肯尼迪都曾派出联邦军队同州国民卫队对峙,对峙的原因是为了实施最高法院黑人学生可以与白人同校的判决。今天,马丁·路德·金已经成为美国乃至全世界人民景仰的对象,但对于他当时所处的艰难环境可能早已淡忘了。权利是需要争取才能得到的,在争取的过程中甚至会与当时的社会环境发生激烈的冲突,以至于像金博士那样付出生命的代价。冲破藩篱、英勇无畏,这就是马丁·路德·金的伟大所在。

观 察 OBSERVATION

## Reading Guidance

　　2011年10月23日,欧元区首脑会议在比利时首都布鲁塞尔的欧盟总部召开。在此次会议上,法德两国就应对欧元区债务危机采取全面有力的解决方案达成一致,具体方案有望在10月26日举行第二次首脑会议上最终通过。四天内两次峰会,欧盟这样不同寻常的会程设置似乎凸显了问题的紧迫复杂。

　　自金融危机爆发以来,主权债务问题此起彼伏。最早出现主权债务危机的国家是冰岛。2009年底,世界著名的三大评级机构(惠誉、穆迪、标普)先后调低了对希腊的主权信用评级。这一举动引发了全球对于希腊债务危机的关注。随后,多国陷入此次危机,欧债危机风暴愈演愈烈。这场危机不像美国次贷危机那样来势汹汹,但其缓慢的进程也牵动着全球经济的神经。在欧元区17国中,以葡萄牙、爱尔兰、意大利、希腊和西班牙五国的债务问题最为严重。

# Europe Rushes to Contain Debt Crisis

　　French, German and Greek leaders are scheduled to hold a conference call Wednesday on how to contain Europe's deepening financial crisis that also is triggering alarm in other continents.

　　The call by leaders of Europe's two largest economies—France and Germa-

ny—to its weakest, Greece, underscores deepening worries about the region's financial troubles.

It comes ahead of a Friday meeting by finance ministers from the 17 nations sharing the euro currency to address a debt crisis that began with Greece, Portugal and Ireland, and now risks dragging in Italy and Spain.

U.S. Treasury Secretary Timothy Geithner is attending the talks for the first time, amid signs the crisis might also spread overseas. In remarks to American news station CNBC, Geithner said European leaders are aware they need to do more to earn international confidence.

Fabian Zuleeg, chief economist at the Brussels-based European Policy Center, says the United States is right to be concerned. "The intervention from the U.S. has also shown, at least a risk that the stability of the financial system as a whole—the global financial system—might be under threat again," he said. "We might have a financial situation where a possible default of Greece might have knock-on effects around the world as well."

Greece is under pressure to make good its austerity promises in return for getting more rescue funds. But analysts believe European governments sharing the euro currency also must agree to closer economic unity if the eurozone is to remain viable.

In remarks before the European Parliament Wednesday, European Commission President Jose Manuel Barroso said the commission will propose creating "Eurobonds" as a way for eurozone governments to jointly guarantee their debts.

"I am convinced we need a deeper and more results-driven integration. And let me be clear, this has to be within the community system. A system based purely on intergovernmental cooperation has not worked in the past and will not work in the future," Barroso stated.

Chances that the eurozone might fall apart were once dismissed as unlikely. Now, analysts like Zuleeg say it's a real possibility. "I don't think a very orderly exit of a single country is a very likely plot. I think it is much more likely that we either have the eurozone holding together or we get a chaotic process where other countries come under pressure as soon as one of the countries, such as Greece, says they can no longer pay their debt," he said.

European leaders converge on Brussels Sunday for a crucial summit aimed at forging a plan to save the euro currency. As Greece struggles to avoid a default on its debts, EU leaders must try to stop the crisis from spreading to much bigger economies like Italy and Spain, which could threaten the future of the European Union itself.

Two days of violent protests and strikes preceded Greece's latest effort to slash government spending. Defying the protesters, Prime Minister Papandreou succeeded in getting the latest round of austerity measures passed in Parliament, vital to secure the next slice of European and IMF bailout money.

That will give encouragement to European leaders. After months of turmoil and credit downgrades, Sunday's summit is billed as the moment Europe must finally come together to stop the tide of its debt crisis. German Chancellor Angela Merkel struck an upbeat tone ahead of the meeting.

"If we want to use the crisis as an opportunity," Merkel said, "if we are determined to have more Europe, then we must seize the crisis as an opportunity and be prepared for unconventional and quicker action."

Few leaders appear confident of a quick agreement; a second summit has already been penciled in for Wednesday next week. By then, France and Germany say they will have bridged their differences on how Europe's bailout fund should be strengthened.

Analysts say the initial focus will be on how to pump more capital into troubled banks. And that's just the start.

Experts say economic growth also is needed for Greece and other debt-strapped nations to rebound.

Tim Ohlenburg of London analyst group the Center for Economic and Busi-

ness Research says more radical measures are needed for investors to regain confidence in Europe.

"We think there's hope for the eurozone in the long term overall if Europe manages to put a new institutional framework in place and manages either to let go of economies that are not viable in the euro, or find a transfer mechanism," said Ohlenburg.

No eurozone leader dares to talk in public of weaker members dropping the currency. But the only alternative, says Olehnburg, is a truly federal Europe.

"I think the only way to put an end to this situation, in general, is treaty change," added Ohlenburg. "More power to Europe, closer integration, fiscal union."

Such is the gravity of its debt crisis that Europe's very foundations are up for debate.

## Notes

austerity:（经济的）紧缩
chaotic:混乱的
slash:大幅度削减
bailout:紧急(财政)援助
turmoil:骚动,混乱,动乱
fiscal:（政府）财政的

# 欧洲加紧遏制债务危机

法国、德国和希腊的领导人星期三举行电话会议,商讨如何遏制欧洲日益加深的财务危机,此次危机也给其他大洲敲响警钟。

欧洲最大的两个经济体法国和德国以及欧洲最弱的经济体希腊的领导人举行电话会议,凸显了对该地区财政问题的忧虑日益加深。

稍后,欧元区17国财政部长将于星期五举行会议,商讨解决债务危机。这场危机始于希腊、葡萄牙和爱尔兰,而现在,意大利和西班牙也面临被卷入债务危机的风险。

美国财长盖特纳将首次参加欧元区财长会议,有迹象显示这次危机也可能扩散到欧洲之外。盖特纳在美国消费者新闻与商业频道(CNBC)电视台发表的讲话中说,欧洲领导人知道他们需要采取更多行动以赢得国际社会的信心。

位于布鲁塞尔的欧洲政策中心首席经济学家法比安·祖里格说,美国感到担忧是对的。祖里格说:"美国的介入也表明,作为一个整体的金融系统的稳定性面临风险,全球金融系统可能再次受到威胁。希腊可能对其债务违约,这种财政状况也可能在全球产生连锁反应。"

希腊迫于压力履行其做出的财政紧缩承诺,以此获得更多的援助资金。但分析人士认为,如果欧元区想要继续以现有方式运作下去,欧元区国家政府还必须同意进行更大的经济整合。

欧盟委员会主席巴罗佐星期三向欧洲议会发表讲话称,欧盟委员会将提议创建"欧洲债券",这是整个欧元区共同担保的政府债券。

巴罗佐说:"我相信,我们需要程度更深、更注重结果的整合。说清楚一点就是这必须是欧元区系统内的整合。一个完全是基于政府间合作的系统过去没有产生过效用,将来也是没有效用的。"

欧元区分裂的可能性曾一度被认为是不可能的。然而现在,像祖里格这样的分析人士说,这真的是可能的。祖里格说:"我认为不太可能出现单个国家非常有序地退出欧元区这种情况,我认为更可能发生的情形是,要么欧元区仍凝聚在一起,要么就会出现一个混乱的过程,即只要一个国家,比如希腊说它们无法再偿还债务,其他国家就会受到压力。"

欧洲国家领导人将于星期天在布鲁塞尔举行一个重要峰会,目的在于制定一项拯救欧元的计划。在希腊艰难地设法避免债务违约之际,欧盟领导人必须设法防止这场危机扩散到意大利和西班牙等更大的经济体。如果危机扩散,可能威胁到欧盟的未来。

在希腊推进削减政府开支的新一轮努力之前,民众进行了为期两天的暴力抗议和罢工。希腊总理帕潘德里欧无视抗议者的要求,成功地使最新一轮的财政紧缩方案在议会通过,这对希腊获得欧盟和国际货币基金组织(IMF)提供的下一笔援助金至关重要。

这将给欧洲领导人带来鼓舞。在经过几个月的混乱和信用评级下降之后,星期天的峰会成为欧洲必须最终团结一致遏制债务危机蔓延的时刻。德国总理默克尔在此次峰会前夕发出积极的呼声。

默克尔说:"如果我们想利用这次危机作为一个机会,如果我们决心想要一个更加整合的欧洲,我们就必须抓住这次危机带来的机会,准备采取非常规的、更迅速的行动。"

看来很少有欧洲领导人对迅速达成协议抱有信心。欧盟定于下星期三举行第二次峰会。法国和德国表示,届时它们将就如何加强欧洲的援助基金弥合分歧。

分析人士说,初步的一个重点将在于如何向陷入困境的银行注入更多资金,而这只是开始。

专家指出,希腊和其他深陷债务危机的国家还需要经济增长来实现反弹。伦敦的分析机构经济和商业研究中心的蒂姆·欧伦伯格说,需要采取更多激进的措施,使投资者对欧洲重拾信心。

观察 OBSERVATION

　　欧伦伯格说："我们认为,如果欧洲能够实行新的机构框架,能够放弃不适合采用欧元的国家或者找到一项转移机制,从长期来讲,欧元区总体上是有希望的。"没有哪个欧元区领导人敢公开谈论让较弱的成员国放弃欧元。欧伦伯格说,"唯一的替代办法是构建一个真正联合的欧洲。我认为结束当前这种状况的唯一办法是修改欧盟条约,给欧洲带来更大的力量,更深度的整合,构建财政联盟。"

　　此次债务危机如此严重,以至于要讨论欧洲的根基问题。

**More to Read**

　　欧洲国家主权债务危机的不断蔓延让人们不禁要问,欧洲怎么了?到底是什么原因致使原本处于世界经济发展前列的欧洲区变得如此混乱不堪?学者们认为,政府失职、过度举债、制度缺陷等问题的累积效应最终导致了这场危机的爆发。然而,这些所谓的长期性问题难道从来就没有人发现吗?早在冰岛危机爆发的时候,就已有人预言,冰岛绝不是最后一个出问题的国家。在这个以银行业为国民经济主要支柱的国家,主权评级下调无疑是致命一击,这意味着这个国家以主权为担保的债务有可能无法偿还,存在那里的钱有可能都打了水漂。而在类似于冰岛这样的国家,由于实体经济发展受到各种条件的限制,虚拟经济成为发展的首要领域。在虚拟经济发展带动下的高消费、高福利为其国内民众带来了舒适的生活,然而一旦虚拟经济无法支撑,这些原有的待遇有会变成沉重的负担。因此,我们必须反思,现有的发展模式真是人们需要的吗?

## Reading Guidance

印度作为人口大国，近几年成为世界上发展最快的经济体之一。印度作为南亚地区无可争议的龙头国家，经过20年的经济改革后，世人已不再追问它是否能够崛起，而是它什么时候会崛起。它现在已经是广被看好的"金砖国家"之一。

在印度经济史上，1991年是特殊的一年。印度爆发了国际收支危机。那年，在时任财政部长辛格的主导下，印度政府开始全力推行举世瞩目的以"自由化、市场化、全球化和私有化"为特色的、被称为"四化"的新经济政策。这些改革措施的最终结果是显著的，印度政府大幅度减少了对企业的干涉，并对外国直接投资表现出了更为积极的态度。从1991年以来，印度经济以平均每年5.9%的速度增长，2004年第一季度，印度经济增长达到了有史以来最快的10.4%。但是20年过后，印度的贫富差距依然存在。这个南亚国家需要极力缩小兴旺的中产阶级与数百万贫困者之间的差距。

## 20 Years On: Economic Reform in India

Two decades ago, India opened up its tightly regulated economy, unleashing a wave of reforms that transformed the country and put it in the league of the world's fastest growing economies. But many consider the job only partially complete and say the South Asian country needs to bridge the gap between a prosperous middle class and the millions of people who still grapple with poverty.

Rajeev Nanda, a software professional, was among a wave of young people who migrated to the United States in the 1980s, because of a lack of job opportunities at home. In 2001, a decade after India opened its socialist-style economy, he returned to establish an office in Bangalore for the U.S.—based company that employed him.

Nanda found a country dramatically different from the one he had left 12 years before. "When we went, it was a one-way ticket to the U.S.," explained Nanda. "Then the economy opened up. The opportunities created a different mindset. Suddenly there was a lot of hope and lot of excitement in the air."

The liberalization drive launched in 1991 came at a time when India was confronting a crisis. It was on the verge of defaulting on its international debt.

Prime Minister Manmohan Singh—then the country's finance minister—lifted restrictions on foreign investors, relaxed stifling controls on domestic industry and slashed taxes. The results were soon evident. India's economy became the world's second fastest-growing economy, after China. Led by a thriving information-technology sector, the services sector boomed. Manufacturing industries expanded. Exports flourished. A huge middle class emerged.

The head of the Federation of Indian Chambers of Commerce and Industry, Rajiv Kumar, says the unshackling of the private sector created the economic boom. "The most important thing in my view is to have freed the Indian entrepreneurial spirit, which is its traditional strength. It had been chained and caged prior to 1991 in the ideology of central planning and socialism etc," Kumar said.

But, 20 years later, analysts say India's economic revolution is only partially complete. And, some people worry that it is running out of steam.

For years, investors have waited for a second wave of reforms to open up sectors which are still tightly regulated, such as retail and insurance. Busines-

ses grapple with lack of infrastructure, as everything from power generation to the transportation network falls short. Several Indian companies are investing overseas, rather than at home where they are deterred by problems such as acquiring land for factories.

But economists say even more pressing is the problem of unequal growth. While one half of the country prospers, the other half continues to grapple with poverty. In the cities, gated residential complexes and gleaming shopping malls contrast with sprawling urban slums.

Poverty is rampant in many backward, rural regions. A little more than 40 percent of the people—about 450 million—live on less than $2 a day.

Top Indian officials are confident the problem can be addressed by even faster growth. Among them is Home Minister P. Chidambaram, who was formerly finance minister. "Our biggest failure is that the pace of reduction of poverty has not been fast enough, that the growth of employment has not been fast enough," Chidambaram said. "The pace of reduction of poverty must pick up and that can only happen if growth averages over eight percent and is sustained at nine percent for several years."

But there are worries that brisk economic growth may not be enough to address problems such as lack of access to schooling and health care for millions of Indians. Rates of malnourishment and infant mortality are among the worst in the world. Millions of children are still unschooled.

A top Indian economist, Swaminathan Aiyar, blames lack of effective governance for such problems. "It is not enough to say there is some economic growth. I mean what is the condition of your schools? What is the condition of your public health? What is the condition of government services in general? That is the biggest problem that is crying out," noted Aiyar.

Analysts also say that, in the past year, economic issues have been put on the back burner as the government focuses its energies on fighting allegations of huge official corruption. They say this has led to a policy paralysis in the government.

Minister Chidambaram says the country needs to put the focus back on the economy to realize its full potential. "The center stage must once again be restored to growth, to change, to reforms, better governance. So what you see today in declining investment or more foreign outward investment, all these can be resolved... and then outpace even China, that's not impossible, people are beginning to talk about outpacing China," Chidambaram said.

Rajeev Nanda says that, two decades after liberalization, most professionals would rather stay in India than migrate to Western countries. "In the last few years, I have seen even a reverse, where people do not want to go. They are simply having a better life, better opportunities right here," Nanda said.

Economists say the challenge in the coming years will be to bridge the gap between the middle class and the poor, so that those living now in urban slums and the countryside can echo the same sentiment.

## Notes

unleashing: 解除……的束缚, 释放
grapple: 扭打, 格斗; 设法解决
unshackling: 释放; 解去……的枷锁
rampant: 猖獗的, 蔓延的, 猛烈的
malnourishment: 营养不良

# 印度经济改革20年

20年前,印度开放了严格管制的经济,展开了一波改革浪潮,使该国实现转型并成为世界上增长最快的经济体之一。但许多人认为这一改革工程只完成了一部分,他们说,这个南亚国家需要缩小兴旺的中产阶级与数百万贫困者之间的差距。

拉吉夫·南达是一名软件专业人士,20世纪80年代他因为印度国内缺乏工作机会随着年轻人移民浪潮移民到美国。2001年,也就是印度开放其社会主义式的经济10年之后,他回到印度,在班加罗尔设立了他所任职的美国公司的印度办事处。

南达发现,与他12年前离开时相比,这个国家发生了巨大的变化。南达说:"当年我们去美国时,买的是单程机票。之后,印度经济开放了。这些机遇造就了不同的心情。突然之间充满了很多希望,到处洋溢着兴奋的情绪。"

1991年开始推行经济自由化之时印度正在应付一场危机。当时该国正处于对其国际债务违约的边缘。

当时担任财政部长的现任总理曼莫汉·辛格,取消了对外国投资者的限制,放松了对国内产业令人窒息的管制,并实行减税。改革的效果很快显现。印度成为世界上增长第二快的经济体,仅次于中国。受繁荣的信息技术产业的带动,服务业兴旺,制造业扩张,出口旺盛,出现了大规模的中产阶级。

印度工商联合会秘书长拉吉夫·库马尔说,私营部门的开放造就了经济繁荣。库马尔说:"我认为最重要的一点是印度的创业精神得到解放,创业精神是印度的传统优势。在1991年以前,这种精神受到中央计划和社会主义等理念的束缚。"

不过,分析人士说,到20年之后的今天,印度的经济革命只完成了一部分。一些人担心这一进程正失去动力。

多年来,投资者们一直在等待新一轮的经济改革,开放现在仍然管制严格的领域,例如:零售业和保险业。企业苦于基础设施的缺乏,与发电和运输网络相关的一切事情都满足不了需要。多个印度公司都在海外投资,因为在国内受到太多问题的阻碍,比如说:需要建设厂房用地。

但是经济学家说更严重的问题是经济增长不均衡。国家的这边繁荣兴旺,那边却还在与贫困抗争。城市里,保安严密的住宅社区、灯火通明的购物中心,与乱七八糟的贫民窟形成鲜明的对比。

在许多落后的农村地区,贫困问题非常严重。40%多一点的人——也就是大约4.5亿人每天的生活费用不到2美元。

印度的高级官员相信,更快的经济增长能够解决这个问题。内政部长奇丹巴拉姆就持这种观点,他曾经担任财政部长。奇丹巴拉姆说:"我们最大的失败就是减少贫困的步伐不够快,就业的增长不够快。减少贫困的步伐必须加快,而只有经济增长率平均超过8%、连续几年保持9%,减贫步伐才能加快。"

然而,人们担心经济的快速增长可能不足以解决数百万印度民众缺乏教育和医疗服务等这类问题。印度的营养不良率和婴儿死亡率是世界最高者之一。数百万儿童仍然失学。

印度著名经济学家斯瓦米纳森·艾亚尔将这些问题归因于缺乏有效的治理。艾亚尔说:"只有一些经济增长是不够的。我的意思是学校的条件怎么样?公共医疗的条件如何?政府服务的总体状况怎样?这是正被大声疾呼的最大问题。"

分析人士也指出,过去一年,经济问题已被置于脑后,印度政府专注于应对官员严重腐败的指控。分析人士说,这已导致政府的政策瘫痪。

内政部长奇丹巴拉姆表示,印度需要重新专注于经济,以实现全部潜力。奇丹巴拉姆说:"中心任务必须再次回到增长、改变、改革,以及更好的治理。如此一来,你现在看到的投资下降或外向的外国投资增加,所有这些问题都能解决……甚至能够超过中国,这不是不可能的,人们已经在开始谈论印度将超过中国。"

拉吉夫·南达说,印度经济自由化20年后,大多数专业人士都愿意留在印度,而不是移民到西方国家。南达说:"过去这几年,我看到了相反的情况,人们不想离开。他们在这里就有更好的生活,更好的机会。"

经济学家说,未来几年的挑战将是缩小中产阶级与穷人之间的差距,这样一来,那些现在住在城市贫民窟和农村的人们也能够有同样的兴奋情绪。

## More to Read

印度是一个对中国人来说充满了矛盾感情的国度。回顾历史,两国间的思想文化交流源远流长,唐玄奘西天取经的故事在中国更是妇孺皆知。然而,自从1962年边界冲突之后,中印两国在政治和军事上的对峙和竞争延续至今。现在,随着印度经济的起飞,不少西方人认为,21世纪地缘竞争最为激烈的将是"龙"与"象"的争斗。近20年的印度经济改革使其越来越有挑战中国的潜力。但另一方面,印度自身也存在很多难以根除的痼疾——贫富分化严重、民族以及宗教冲突等问题始终无法得到解决。这些问题都将直接制约印度的发展速度与趋势。

观 察 OBSERVATION

## Reading Guidance

每年的 11 月 14 日是世界糖尿病日。近年来,随着世界各国社会经济的发展和居民生活水平的提高,糖尿病的发病率及患病率逐年升高,成为威胁人民健康的重大社会问题,引起各国政府、卫生部门以及广大医务工作者的关注和重视。按照世界卫生组织(WHO)及国际糖尿病联盟(IDF)专家组的建议,糖尿病可分为Ⅰ型、Ⅱ型、其他特殊类型及妊娠糖尿病 4 种。目前世界糖尿病患者人数最多的前 3 位国家为印度、中国、美国。Ⅱ型糖尿病是糖尿病人群的主体,占糖尿病患者的 90% 左右。糖尿病患病率最高的地区是太平洋岛国瑙鲁(Nauru)和美国皮玛(Pima)印第安人。发病率增加最快的是由穷到富急剧变化着的发展中国家。导致糖尿病多发的原因有遗传因素、平均寿命延长、生活水平提高、不健康的生活方式和肥胖等。

## Study Shows Diabetes Surging Worldwide

The number of adults worldwide with diabetes has more than doubled in the past three decades—jumping to nearly 350 million. And it continues to surge, according to a new study in the journal Lancet. Researchers say much of this dramatic increase—in Pacific island countries, North America and some of

the Gulf states—is due to aging populations and rapid population growth. But part of it has also been driven by rising obesity rates, especially among young people.

Dr. Staten, a senior adviser for the Diabetes Research Division at the National Institutes of Health, said, "One of the big concerns of diabetes today is that diabetes did not occur in children 30 years ago, or it was rarely seen. But as children in America have become heavier, we are now starting to recognize it in children, especially in children of minority populations, largely African-American and Hispanic."

It's documented: diabetes is a global problem. A new study shows that one in 10 adults, in countries throughout the world, suffers from diabetes.

Goodarz Danaei, is a researcher at the Harvard School of Public Health and one of the study's authors: "What our study shows is that it is no longer a disease of the affluent countries."

Researchers collected data on blood sugar levels from nearly three million people in 200 countries over a 30-year period. Most of the participants had Type-II diabetes, a disease linked to aging, obesity and inactivity.

Type II diabetes weakens the body's ability to use insulin, the hormone that regulates blood sugar, which can damage the heart, eyes, kidneys and nerves People with diabetes cannot control their blood sugar levels. This can lead to heart disease and stroke, disability and early death.

The study found that there are nearly 350 million people with diabetes in the world and almost 140 million live in India and China, 40 percent of all cases worldwide.

Even in countries where diabetes is not rampant, populations have increased and so, too, has the number of diabetics.

"Even if only two percent or one percent of the population is diabetic, but you have more than a billion people in your country, the sheer number of diabetes patients will drive the costs and resources that the health systems have to put into disease control and management," Dr. Danaei said.

About 26 million people in the U.S have diabetes, and nearly 90 percent of these cases are Type II diabetes. According to the U.S. Centers for Disease Control and Prevention the cost of diabetes in the United States is about $174 billion per year, mostly for treatment of complications and disabilities.

Diabetes is one of the most expensive diseases to treat because it requires long term care—not just to regulate blood sugar levels, but to deal with its serious medical complications. The World Health Organization estimates that more than 70 percent of people with diabetes live in low and middle income countries. Many people in these countries cannot afford to buy the medications they need to control their diabetes and neither can countries with already slim public health budgets.

The WHO projects that if current trends continue, deaths from the disease could double by 2030, and health experts warn it could become a global epidemic, with significant health and economic consequences.

"They have to find cost-effective ways to either prevent the disease or diagnose the disease at an earlier stage or treat the complication of diabetes in a much more effective manner," said Dr. Danaei.

This study confirms what doctors are already seeing in their clinics, doctors like Betul Hatipolu at the Cleveland Clinic.

"It is not a surprise for us," she said. "When we practice every day, we see so many new cases, I'm not surprised at all."

The authors say countries need to aggressively promote healthy lifestyles. That's also what doctors who treat this disease are saying.

"I would just love to tell everybody that they have to exercise and they have to eat healthier, otherwise everyone is at risk to develop diabetes," Dr. Hatipolu said.

The study's authors say diabetes is likely to be one of the defining features of global health needs unless public health campaigns to prevent it are success-

ful.

  Scientists say obesity and lack of exercise contribute to the increased number of cases. There is no known cure for diabetes, but doctors say making lifestyle changes—such as maintaining a healthy weight by eating right and exercising—is the best way to treat and prevent it.

**Notes**

  diabetes：糖尿病
  surge：猛增
  obesity：肥胖
  affluent：富裕的，富足的
  rampant：猖獗的，遏制不住的
  epidemic：流行病

# 研究表明糖尿病正冲击全球

  在过去的30多年里，全世界成年糖尿病人的数量已经翻了一倍还多。根据医学杂志《柳叶刀》的一项新研究表明，这个数字还在继续增加。研究人员说，在太平洋岛国、北美洲和一些海湾国家，糖尿病人明显增多的最主要原因是人口老龄化和人口的迅速增长。还有部分原因是不断上升的肥胖率，尤以年轻人居多。

  美国国家卫生署糖尿病研究部的高级顾问史坦顿医生说，"当前有关糖尿病最大的担忧之一是30年前糖尿病并不出现在儿童身上，或者说极少发现儿童病例。但是随着美国儿童体重的上升,我们现在开始在儿童,尤其是少数族裔儿童——主要是非洲裔和拉美裔身上发现糖尿病病例。"

文献记载,糖尿病是全球性的问题。一项新的研究课题显示,全世界各国中有十分之一的成年人患有糖尿病。

这项研究的成员之一,哈佛大学公共卫生学院研究者古达孜·丹纳依说:"我们的研究表明,糖尿病不再是专属于富裕国家的疾病。"

研究人员在30年间从200个国家近300万人中采集血糖指标数据。绝大多数参与者都是Ⅱ型糖尿病患者,患有Ⅱ型糖尿病与老龄、肥胖和不常运动有关。

Ⅱ型糖尿病会削弱人体使用胰岛素(控制血糖的荷尔蒙)的能力,从而损坏心脏、眼睛、肾脏和神经。糖尿病人不能控制他们的血糖水平,就有可能患上心脏病、中风、残疾和早逝。

研究发现,在将近3.5亿的糖尿病人群中,有1.4亿人生活在印度和中国,占全世界病案的40%。

即使在糖尿病并不严重的国家,人口的增加同样也使糖尿病患者的数量增多。

丹纳依医生说:"即使糖尿病人只占人口数的2%或1%,但对于超过10亿人口的国家来说,糖尿病患者的绝对数量会驱使国家医疗系统不得不加大疾病控制与管理的费用和资源投入。"

在美国,2600万人患有糖尿病,而且将近90%的病例都是Ⅱ型糖尿病。美国疾病控制预防中心透露,美国每年在糖尿病上的投入大约为1740亿美元,主要用于并发症和残疾的治疗。

糖尿病是治疗费用最昂贵的疾病之一,因为它需要长期治疗——不仅要控制血糖水平,还要对严重的并发症进行治疗。据世界卫生与健康组织估算,超过70%的糖尿病患者居住在中低等收入国家。许多这样的病人买不起控制糖尿病病情所需的药物,而他们国家的公共健康经费预算非常微薄,所以也帮不上什么忙。

世界卫生组织指出,这种状况如果持续下去的话,到2030年,糖尿病的死亡人数将增加一倍。健康专家提醒说,在不可忽视的健康状况和经济状况的双重作用下,糖尿病有可能成为一种全球流行病。

"他们必须找到合算的办法,争取做到预防糖尿病、早期诊断糖尿病和更加有效地治疗糖尿病并发症。"

这项研究也证实了医生们在诊所里所了解到的情况。克利夫兰诊所的贝杜尔·海蒂波露医生就是其中的一个。

"对此,我们并不吃惊。"贝杜尔·海蒂波露医生说,"在每天的临床实践中,我们接触到太多的新病例,所以我一点儿都不惊讶。"

研究者提出,各个国家都需要强有力地倡导健康的生活方式。这也是糖尿病医生所期望的。

海蒂波露医生说:"我现在只想告诉大家必须要锻炼身体和健康饮食,否则,每个人都面临患上糖尿病的危险。"

该研究报告称,糖尿病有可能成为全球健康状况的表征之一,除非公共卫生活动能够做到成功地预防糖尿病。

科学家们说肥胖和缺乏运动促使了糖尿病病例的增加。到目前为止,糖尿病还是不能完全治愈的疾病。但医生说,改变生活方式是治疗和预防糖尿病最好的办法——做到合理饮食和合理锻炼,从而保持健康的体重。

## More to Read

在现代社会,随着人类生活水平的普遍提高,"富裕病"与"穷人病"成为了一对密切相关的概念。所谓"富裕病"是指纵向比较而言,随着人们摄入动物性食品的数量比以前更多,但运动量明显降低,结果导致整个人类群体中肥胖以及心血管疾病等"富裕"疾病显著增加。然而横向来看,如果按人的收入情况进行划分,我们会发现在低收入群体中罹患上述疾病的比例要高于高收入人群,这就是"穷人病"的由来。究其原因,除了在一些发达国家"菜比肉贵"之外,健康意识的作用可能更为关键——富人们接受健康信息的渠道更多,也有钱从事"昂贵"的健身运动、雇佣专业的健康顾问。总之,健康已经越来越超出医疗保健本身,变成更具有社会特征的问题。

观察 OBSERVATION

## Reading Guidance

史蒂夫·乔布斯(1955~2011),发明家、企业家、美国苹果公司联合创办人、前行政总裁。1976年乔布斯和朋友成立苹果电脑公司,亲历了苹果公司数十年的起落与兴衰,先后领导和推出了麦金塔计算机、iMac、iPod、iPhone等风靡全球的电子产品,深刻地改变了现代通讯、娱乐乃至生活方式。2011年10月5日他因病逝世,享年56岁。乔布斯是改变世界的天才,他凭着敏锐的触觉和过人的智慧,勇于变革,不断创新,引领了全球资讯科技和电子产品的潮流,把电脑和电子产品变得简约化、平民化,让曾经是昂贵稀罕的电子产品成为现代人生活的一部分。2011年8月24日,乔布斯向苹果董事会提交辞呈,乔布斯在信中并没有指明辞职原因,但这一时期他一直都在与胰腺癌做斗争。此篇报道选自《纽约时报》,在乔布斯辞职之后,对他的奋斗之路做出了深刻的诠释。

# Reaping the Rewards of Risk-Taking

Since Steven P. Jobs resigned as chief executive of Apple last Wednesday, much has been said about him as a peerless corporate leader who has created immense wealth for shareholders, and guided the design of hit products that are transforming entire industries, like music and mobile communications.

All true, but let's think different, to borrow the Apple marketing slogan of years back. Let's look at Mr. Jobs as a role model.

Above all, he is an innovator. His creative force is seen in products like the iPod, iPhone and iPad, and in new business models for pricing and distributing music and mobile software online. Studies of innovation come to the same conclusion: you can't engineer innovation, but you can increase the odds of it occurring. And Mr. Jobs's career can be viewed as a consistent pursuit of improving those odds, both for himself and the companies he has led Mr. Jobs, of course, has enjoyed singular success. But innovation, broadly defined, is the crucial ingredient in all economic progress—higher growth for nations, more competitive products for companies, and more prosperous careers for individuals. And Mr. Jobs, experts say, personifies what works in the innovation game.

"We can look at and learn from Steve Jobs what the essence of American innovation is," says John Kao, an innovation consultant to corporations and governments.

Many other nations, Mr. Kao notes, are now ahead of the United States in producing what are considered the raw materials of innovation. These include government financing for scientific research, national policies to support emerging industries, educational achievement, engineers and scientists graduated, even the speeds of Internet broadband service.

Yet what other nations typically lack, Mr. Kao adds, is a social environment that encourages diversity, experimentation, risk-taking, and combining skills from many fields into products that he calls "recombinant mash-ups," like the iPhone, which redefined the smartphone category.

"The culture of other countries doesn't support the kind of innovation that Steve Jobs exemplifies, as America does," Mr. Kao says.

Workers of every rank are told these days that wide-ranging curiosity and continuous learning are vital to thriving in the modern economy. Formal education matters, career counselors say, but real-life experience is often even more valuable.

An adopted child, growing up in Silicon Valley, Mr. Jobs displayed those traits early on. He was fascinated by electronics as a child, building Heathkit do-it-yourself projects, like radios.

Mr. Jobs dropped out of Reed College after a semester and trekked around India in search of spiritual enlightenment, before returning to Silicon Valley to found Apple with his friend, Stephen Wozniak, an engineering wizard. Mr. Jobs was forced out of Apple in 1985, went off and founded two other companies, Next and Pixar, before returning to Apple in 1996 and becoming chief executive in 1997.

His path was unique, but innovation experts say the pattern of exploration is not unusual. "It's often people like Steve Jobs who can draw from a deep reservoir of diverse experience that generate breakthrough ideas and insights," says Hal B. Gregersen, a professor at the European Institute of Business Administration, or insead.

Mr. Gregersen is a co-author of a new book, *The Innovator's DNA* (Harvard Business School Press), based on an eight-year study of 5,000 entrepreneurs and executives worldwide. His two collaborators and co-authors are Jeff Dyer, a professor at Brigham Young University, and Clayton M. Christensen, a professor at the Harvard Business School, whose 1997 book *The Innovator's Dilemma* popularized the concept of "disruptive innovation".

The academics identify five traits that are common to the disruptive innovators: questioning, experimenting, observing, associating and networking. Their bundle of characteristics echoes the ceaseless curiosity and willingness to take risks noted by other experts. Associating, Mr. Gregersen explains, is the ability to make idea-producing connections by linking concepts from different disciplines—intellectual mash-ups. "Innovators engage in these mental activities regularly," Mr. Gregersen says. "It's a habit."

Innovative companies, according to the authors, typically enjoy higher valuations in the stock market, which they call an "innovation premium." It is calculated by estimating the share of a company's value that cannot be accounted for by its current products and cash flow. The innovation premium tries to quantify investors' bets that a company will do even better in the future because of innovation.

Mr. Gregersen says just as what Jobs has done in his second stint at Apple, without the experience outside the company, especially at Pixar—the computer-animation studio that created a string of critically and commercially successful movies, like '*Toy Story*' and '*Up*'.

Mr. Jobs suggested much the same thing during a commencement address to the graduating class at Stanford in 2005. "It turned out that getting fired from Apple was the best thing that could have ever happened to me," he told the students. Mr. Jobs also spoke of perseverance. "Sometimes life hits you in the head with a brick," he said. "Don't lose faith."

Mr. Jobs ended his commencement talk with a call to innovation, in one's choice of work and in life. Be curious, experiment, take risks, he said. His admonition was punctuated by the words on the back of the final edition of *The Whole Earth Catalog* which he quoted: "Stay hungry. Stay foolish." "And," Mr. Jobs said, "I have always wished that for myself. And now, as you graduate to begin anew, I wish that for you."

## Notes

trek (around): 艰苦跋涉, 长途旅行
reservoir: 水库, 汇聚, 储藏
commencement: 毕业典礼
perseverance: 坚持不懈
admonition: 告诫, 劝告

观察 OBSERVATION

# 播下风险种，收获大苹果

自史蒂夫·乔布斯于上周三辞去苹果公司首席执行官一职后，外界对他的溢美之词不绝于耳：他是举世无双的企业领袖，为股东们创造了巨大的财富，经他指导设计的拳头产品在多个领域掀起了全面革命，如音乐产业和移动通信业。

这些都没错，但让我们借用一下几年前苹果的营销口号——换个方式来思考，让我们以看待榜样的角度来看乔布斯。

首先，他是一位革新家。他的创新力量不仅反映在 iPod、iPhone、iPad 这样的产品中，也体现在为音乐和移动软件进行在线定价和发行这一新型商业模式上。其实人们对创新的研究也得出了相同结论：创新不是精心策划的产物，但可以由此增加其发生的概率。乔布斯的职业生涯可谓是在坚持不懈地为创造更多的创新机会而努力，这既是为了他自己，也是为其麾下的公司。当然，乔布斯享受过非凡的成功。不过广义上的创新其实是所有经济发展必不可缺的组成部分——对国家而言是促进经济增长，对公司而言是提高产品竞争力，对个人而言是打造更辉煌的事业。而专家们说，乔布斯就是创新游戏中制胜的关键。

约翰·考是多家企业和政府的创新顾问，他说："看看史蒂夫·乔布斯，我们可以从他身上学到美国式创新的精髓所在。"

约翰·考又提到，现如今，其他许多国家在生产所谓的创新原材料方面都已位列美国之前，包括政府资助科研，国家政策支持新兴工业，教育成果、工程技术和科研人员辈出，甚至在互联网宽带服务方面也突飞猛进。

但约翰·考补充道，其他国家所缺少的却是像美国一样的具有代表性的社会环境，即鼓励多样性，具有实践性，敢于冒险，融合多领域的技术于一体，从而形成他称之为"重组混搭"的产品，就像苹果手机那样，重新定义了智能手机这一类别。

"其他国家的文化没有像美国那样支持史蒂夫·乔布斯所诠释的创新。"约翰·考说道。

时至今日，各阶层的劳动者都已知晓，要想在现代经济中飞黄腾达，宽泛的好奇心并付出持之以恒的努力是至关重要的。职业咨询师说，正规的教育固然重要，但真实生活所赋予的经验往往是更宝贵的。

乔布斯先生，一个被人收养并在硅谷长大的孩子，在很早的时候就展现出了这些特质。在孩童时期，他就对电学着了迷，创建了类似无线电的希思公司产品的自助项目。

乔布斯在里德学院只读了一个学期就辍学了，随后他远渡重洋到印度去寻求精神世界的启蒙，而后重返硅谷，与他的朋友——工程界的奇才斯蒂芬·沃兹尼亚克创建了苹果公司。1985年，乔布斯被迫离开苹果，并成立了另外两家计算机公司和动画公司，1996年，他重返苹果，并于次年出任总裁。

乔布斯的心路历程是独一无二的，但是创新界专家称这样的探索模式并非与众不同，"像史蒂夫·乔布斯这样的人通常能够从丰富的历练这一深邃的聚源中有所汲取，以此释放出突破性的灵感和洞察力。"欧洲工商管理学院教授哈尔·格雷格森这样说道。

格雷格森教授和他的合作者杨百翰大学的杰夫·代尔教授，以及哈佛商学院的克莱顿·克里斯滕森教授通过对于全世界范围内5000个企业家和总裁历时8年的研究，创作而成新的著作《创新者的DNA》一书。而克莱顿·克里斯滕森教授在1997年出版的《创新者的困境》这一专著则推广了"破坏性创新"的概念。

学者们在研究中认为破坏性革新者具备五大共同特征：善于质疑、试验、观察、联想和建立人脉。这些特质就蕴含在其他专家所描述的拥有无尽的好奇心和乐于冒险的行为之中。格雷格森教授解释说，善于联想是通过连接不同领域的概念以形成创造性想法相互连接的能力——即智慧的混搭。他说:"创新者经常性的进行这样的头脑活动,对于他们来说这是一种习惯。"

三位作者认为,创新性的公司通常都在股市享有较高的定价,他们称之为"创新溢价",是通过估算公司价值的股份计算而来,而公司价值股份又不能通过当前产品和现金流进行说明。"创新溢价"设法确定投资者的投入,即由于创新,公司的前景会更好。

格雷格森教授说,就像乔布斯第二次领导苹果时所做的一切,在公司之外没有经验的领域,尤其是皮克斯电脑动画工作室,却创作了一连串的电影,例如《玩具总动员》和《飞屋环游记》,在商业领域和评论界都获得巨大成功。

乔布斯在2005年斯坦福大学毕业典礼上的演讲也表达了同样的观点:"事后证明,从苹果公司被炒是我这辈子经历的最棒的事情。"他还和同学们谈到了要坚持不懈:"有些时候,生活会拿起一块砖头向你的脑袋上猛拍一下。不要失去信心。"

乔布斯在演讲的最后号召大家在工作和生活中都要有创新精神,要保持好奇心,乐于实践,敢于冒险。他的座右铭来自于《整个地球目录》最后一版封底的一句话:"求知若饥,虚心若愚。"他说:"我总是以此自许。当你们毕业,展开新生活,我也以此期许你们。"

**More to Read**

在过去的40年中,史蒂夫·乔布斯一次又一次预见了未来,并把它付诸实践。乔布斯的热情、信念和才识重新塑造了文明的形态,他将美学至上的设计理念在全世界推广开来。他对简约及便利设计的推崇为他赢得了众多忠实的追随者。史蒂夫的才华、激情和精力是创新的无尽来源,丰富和改善了我们的生活。世界因他而无限美好。如今,美国失去了一个天才,乔布斯的名字将与爱迪生和爱因斯坦一同被铭记。他们的理念将继续改变世界,影响后人。

## Reading Guidance

尤利娅·季莫申科,1960年出生,曾任乌克兰政府总理,2010年2月竞选乌克兰总统失败。2011年10月11日,乌克兰法院判处前总理季莫申科2009年乌俄天然气供应协议案滥用职权罪名成立,决定对其判处7年监禁,并因涉嫌在1996年挪用公款偿还个人公司债务4.05亿美元,对其刑事立案调查。季莫申科在接受记者采访时表示,她从未接触过那笔资金,之所以遭到指控其实是因为她经常批评现在的亲俄政府。她说:"他们是在有组织地恐吓反对派,他们简直视法律于无物。"季莫申科获刑在国际上立即引起轩然大波,美国、欧盟成员国及俄罗斯等国纷纷发表声明为季莫申科鸣不平,认为这一案件"纯粹是由政治原因"引起的。

## Ukraine's Joan of Arc, Whose Conviction Caused Europeans' Dissatisfaction

A Kyiv court has sentenced former Prime Minister Yulia Tymoshenko to seven years in jail for abusing her power in a 2009 gas deal with Russia. The conviction and jail sentence comes just as Ukraine hopes to sign a free trade agreement with the European Union.

Protesters jostled with riot police on the main street of Ukraine's capital as news came that Yulia Tymoshenko had been sentenced to prison and to repay $190 million lost in a gas deal with Russia.

Yulia Tymoshenko seemed a little pallor and far more irritated after her arrest, but still managed to pin her long blonde braid into a perfect crown atop her head for her court appearance. Looking as if she had just walked out of a cabinet meeting, Ukraine's former prime minister sat straight-backed and elegant in one of her famously provocative tight gray dresses. Her icy stare bored straight into the judge whom she'd called "a puppet," precipitating her arrest for being in contempt of court on Aug. 5, during her trial for abuses of power in office—a move designed to rattle her cool, her defenders say.

But in the stuffy courtroom, Tymoshenko's firm voice cut through the air to show she hadn't been broken yet. "I am not going to stand up before you," she thundered at the judge. "That would mean I am kneeling to the mafia." Such obstreperousness, designed to delay the proceedings, has been Tymoshenko's strategy since the beginning of the trial, now in its second month. When she didn't have an opportunity to challenge the court, she hurriedly tweeted to her followers from the bench—where she sat behind a row of muscular special-forces officers—or read news on her iPad.

But Tymoshenko, with her trademark blond peasant braid, also has supporters in Brussels, the seat of the European Union. Last week, with Tymoshenko already in jail for two months, European officials warned Ukraine's government that her conviction would threaten a free trade pact with the European Union.

"The European Union has warned Viktor Yanukovych, the Ukrainian president, that his attempts to finalize a free trade agreement with the bloc would be put in jeopardy if the case went forward, and it ended in a sentence for Yulia Tymoshenko," said Yevgeny Kiselyov who runs a political talk show in Kyiv.

Sweden's Prime Minister Carl Bildt warned recently, as the trial ground through its third month, that "political show trials have no place in our Eu-

rope." On Tuesday, after the court decision, Catherine Ashton, the EU's top foreign affairs official, said from Brussels that the EU is "deeply disappointed" with the verdict.

The verdict comes as Ukraine, the largest nation to emerge from the Soviet Union after Russia, stands poised between Russia and Europe.

After four years of negotiations, Ukraine hopes to sign a free trade agreement with the EU in December. This is to be a first step toward Ukraine eventually joining the EU. But with many Europeans saying the EU has expanded too far, too fast, the trial of Tymoshenko is now a lightning rod for opponents of further eastward expansion.

At the same time, Russia is offering membership in a Kremlin-dominated customs union and deep discounts on gas prices, with no lectures on democracy.

With President Yanokovych scheduled to meet with EU officials in Brussels in 10 days, analysts say fast political footwork will be needed to preserve Ukraine's European option.

Viktor Chumak, director of the Ukrainian Public Policy Institute in Kyiv, says now that President Yanukovych has seen his main political rival humiliated by a court trial and conviction, his supporters in Ukraine's parliament will quickly pass a law to change the penalties under the abuse-of-power statute she was convicted of violating. Violators would no longer serve time in jail and would no longer be barred from running for political office.

Shortly after the verdict was announced President Yanukovych unexpectedly broke his long silence on the Tymoshenko case. Talking to journalists Tuesday, he lamented that it was "a regrettable case, which today is thwarting Ukraine's European integration."

He went on to stress that his government is working to update Ukraine's criminal code. But his supporters will have to move fast. The next session of parliament is October 18, and the president is expected in Brussels on October

20.

Kiselyov, the political analyst, says the government's control of the parliament makes that timetable possible.

"They can always vote the same day and the president can sign the respective legislation on the next day or on the same day," noted Kiselyov.

Some European officials have said Ukraine's leader will not be welcome in Brussels if Tymoshenko is still in jail when he visits.

Tymoshenko believes that the European card is her best one to play. Before the verdict, she announced plans to appeal her conviction to the European Court of Human Rights. As soon as the verdict was announced, a parliamentary supporter flatly announced that Ukraine's trade pact with Europe is now dead.

Meanwhile, in Moscow, some analysts say the verdict closes Ukraine's door to Europe and opens its door to Russia.

The coming weeks may decide the East-West tug of war over Ukraine—perhaps the biggest prize from the old Soviet Union.

## Notes

jostle：挤,推,撞

provocative：刺激性的,挑逗的

verdict：裁决,裁定

thwart：阻挠

# 乌克兰"圣女贞德"获刑引起欧洲不满

  乌克兰首都基辅的法庭因前总理尤里娅·季莫申科于2009年与俄罗斯达成的一项天然气协定,以渎职罪名,判处她7年有期徒刑。这项罪名和刑期的宣判,正当乌克兰希望和欧盟签订自由贸易协定之际。

  当季莫申科被判刑的消息传出来时,乌克兰首都基辅街头上的抗议群众和防暴警察发生冲突。法庭还判决,季莫申科必须偿还乌克兰在与俄罗斯天然气交易中损失的1.9亿美元。

  虽然被捕后尤利娅·季莫申科勃然大怒,脸色略显苍白,但是出庭前她依旧把金黄色的长发辫在头顶盘成一个漂亮的皇冠形,就像刚刚开完一场内阁会议。这位乌克兰的前总理身着一套她标志性的灰色紧身连衣裙,端坐如梨,仪态高雅。她目光所凝之处,冰冷的眼神好像要径直刺入那个被她称做是"一只木偶"的法官。在8月5号对季莫申科任职期间滥用职权的审判中,该法官以藐视法庭为由将其羁押。季莫申科的辩护人称这是在"设计"镇定自若的当事人。

  然而,在闷不透气的审判室内,季莫申科用坚定的、穿透性的声音宣示,她并没有被打倒。"我绝不会在你面前起立,"她怒喝法官,"因为这意味着我向幕后黑手下跪。"此般喧闹法庭意在耽搁庭审,这是季莫申科自一个月前诉讼开始就采取的策略。在无法挑战法庭的空当,季莫申科则坐在一排体格健硕的特种部队军官后的被告席上,争分夺秒地给她的支持者发消息,或者在iPad上看看新闻。

  以金色发辫为标志的季莫申科,在欧盟重镇布鲁塞尔也有支持者。上星期在季莫申科入狱两个月后,欧洲官员警告乌克兰政府,她的定罪将威胁到乌克兰与欧盟之间的自由贸易协定的签订。

在基辅主持一个政论节目的俄罗斯媒体人物叶夫根尼·凯瑟列夫说："欧盟亚曾经向乌克兰总统亚努科维奇发出警告,如果这个案件继续下去,导致季莫申科被判刑,他想与欧盟签订自由贸易协定的愿望就有可能实现不了。"

瑞典首相卡尔·比尔特最近在审判进行到第三个月之际警告说："在我们欧洲,为了政治秀而做出的审判,没有立足余地。"星期二,在基辅法庭宣判的当天,欧盟外交事务负责人凯瑟琳·阿什顿在布鲁塞尔说,欧盟对这项判决深感失望。

乌克兰是前苏联解体后获得独立的最大的前苏联加盟共和国。它处于俄罗斯和欧盟之间,寻求和它们保持平衡关系。

乌克兰和欧盟的自由贸易协定谈判已经长达4年。乌克兰希望双方可以在今年12月签署。这将是乌克兰加入欧盟的第一步。但是欧洲许多人士说,欧盟扩展得太远太快。对季莫申科的审判为那些反对欧盟向东扩展的人士提供了避雷针。

与此同时,俄罗斯表示可以让乌克兰获得克里姆林宫主导的关税同盟成员国的资格,以及超低的油价。

乌克兰总统亚努科维奇将于10天后在布鲁塞尔和欧盟官员会晤。分析人士说,他的紧急要务,将是设法保住乌克兰加入欧盟的机会。

基辅乌克兰公共政策研究所主任朱马克说,现在亚努科维奇总统看到他的主要政敌,受到被审判和定罪的羞辱。他在乌克兰议会中的支持者,将很快通过法律,修改有关对滥用职权罪的惩罚规定。新法将规定,触犯这项条例者不必入狱服刑,并且不再被禁止竞选公职。

季莫申科的判决宣布后不久,亚努科维奇总统出人意料地打破他对本案的沉默态度。他星期二对记者谈话时,沉痛表示这个案子令人遗憾,如今瓦解了乌克兰和欧盟的凝聚力。

亚努科维奇还强调,他的政府正努力修正乌克兰的刑事法典。不过,他的支持者的步调必须加快。乌克兰议会将在10月18日开会。亚努科维奇总统将于20日抵达布鲁塞尔。

政治分析家凯瑟列夫说,由于政府控制议会的能力,这个时间表是可以做到的。

他说:"他们总可以在提案的同一天进行表决,总统就在表决当天或第二天签署生效。"

有些欧盟官员说,如果乌克兰领导人前来布鲁塞尔访问时,季莫申科还在狱中的话,他将不会受到欢迎。

季莫申科相信,欧盟是她手中最好的一张牌。在判决之前,她声称将向欧洲人权法庭提出上诉。判决宣布之后,她在乌克兰议会里的一名支持者宣称,乌克兰和欧盟的自由贸易协定已经死亡。

同时在莫斯科,有些分析人士说,这项判决关闭了乌克兰通往欧洲的门户,却打开了与俄罗斯交往之门。

未来一个星期,将是东西方争取乌克兰的关键期。乌克兰可能是来自前苏联的最大的奖品。

## More to Read

判决季莫申科使乌克兰政府受到前所未有的来自国际社会各方的巨大压力。分析人士指出,造成这种局面的主要原因是判决触及了一些国家的政治经济利益。乌克兰欧洲研究院负责人米洛年科认为,如果这一判决成立,将对乌克兰、俄罗斯和欧盟三者的关系产生重大影响。可以肯定的是,乌克兰原定在2011年年底前与欧盟签署联系成员国协议和建立自由贸易区协议的计划将成为泡影。不过他说,这同时也将会为乌俄加强关系带来契机。也就是说,乌克兰在将来可能考虑加入俄罗斯倡导的关税同盟和欧亚联盟。

观察 OBSERVATION

## Reading Guidance

鲁伯特·默多克,美国著名的新闻和媒体经营者,目前是全球庞大传媒帝国新闻集团的主要股东、董事长兼行政总裁。以股票市值来计算,新闻集团已是世界上最大的跨国媒体集团,亦称为"默多克的传媒帝国"。日前,新闻集团旗下的《世界新闻报》由于曝出非法截取、窃听私人电话信息的丑闻而被迫关停,由此也把这位世界报业大亨推到了风口浪尖。新闻集团这次丑闻,势必将影响全球媒体的价值理念和行为准则,公众对媒体的认知也可能因此产生混乱,甚至,这也可能成为政客收紧媒体管制的口实。外界普遍认为,默多克能够面临的最好结局是就此停止在英国市场的发展步伐,而最坏的结局将是其全球范围内的业务都会面临类似在英国遭遇的指控。

## How to Lose Friends And Alienate People?

Two weeks ago News Corporation was a corporate giant led by a legend and on the verge of the biggest deal in its history. Now the deal is off and Rupert Murdoch is widely derided. Britain's three big political parties have ganged up on the company, along with the Church of England, every other media outlet and an array of celebrities. A once-feared colossus has become a pantomime villain, hissed from the stage.

News Corporation has been brought low by allegations that *The News of the World*, one of its British tabloids, paid the police for information and hacked into the voice-mail accounts of many people, some famous, some in tragic circumstances. The implications for British politics, and for the conduct and freedoms of the British press, will take a long time to play out. The corporate impacts already look grieved.

Newspapers are not central to what News Corporation does. In the year to June 2010 they accounted for just 13% of its profits—down from more than 30% nine years earlier. The firm's British newspaper outfit, News International, adds only crumbs to that small slice. News Group Newspapers, the subsidiary that runs *The News of the World* and *The Sun*, has gone from being substantially profitable to being marginally profitable. *The Times* and *The Sunday Times* collectively lose money.

But newspapers are central to who Mr. Murdoch is. News Corporation executives speak with bemusement or despair of the boss's obsession with what goes in his papers, down even to the placement of stories. They are also the source of his extensive political influence in Britain. Most British newspapers are predictably partisan. News International's papers combine a lot of readers with a willingness to swing both ways.

If the damage from the scandal was limited to British newspapers, or even to Mr. Murdoch's reputation and political influence, it would be manageable for the company even if dire for him. It spreads beyond that. Police investigations and a public inquiry loom. News Corporation's leadership and succession, never exactly certain, now seem decidedly wobbly. And the collapse of the bid for BSkyB, a satellite broadcaster, has wrecked a scheme intended to transform the company. News Corporation is no longer free to develop in the way it had planned to, nor necessarily under the leadership did it expect.

观 察 OBSERVATION

A protester wearing a giant Rupert Murdoch mask was parading in front of the media boss's London home this week dressed as a convict. For the man himself it surely will not come to that; for others it quite possibly will. British coppers are investigating both phone-hacking and bribery charges. They told Parliament on July 12th that they have informed 170 people out of almost 4,000 whose names appear in papers seized in 2006 from Glenn Mulcaire, a private investigator formerly employed by *The News of the World*. Just a small fraction of Mr. Mulcaire's prodigious workload could provide the wherewithal for a lot of criminal prosecutions and civil suits. Companies can be found guilty under Britain's Regulation of Investigatory Powers Act if it is proved that criminal behavior like phone-hacking took place with managers' "consent or connivance".

American politicians, aggrieved at claims that victims of terrorism were targeted, are calling for investigations. Some have asked the Department of Justice to consider a probe under the Foreign Corrupt Practices Act, a broad law that targets bribes paid anywhere in the world. But Danforth Newcomb, a lawyer, points out that the law focuses on bribes paid to "obtain or retain" business: it isn't clear whether paying police officers for information would qualify. Another reason for the Americans to stay their hands is that the British can do a perfectly good job of prosecuting bribery by themselves. A new Bribery Act came into force on July 1.

A judicial inquiry into phone-hacking could also do a lot of damage. High-profile public inquiries punch far above their legal weight: they often lead to resignations. This one seems likely to show that both News International and News Corporation made a poor fist of investigating the wrongdoing at *The News of the World*. An internal investigation of e-mails was carried out in 2007, following the convictions of Clive Goodman, the paper's royal editor, and Mr. Mulcaire. Executives later told Parliament they had found nothing to suggest phone-hacking had been widespread. The company's e-mails did, however, apparently contain evidence that bribes had been paid to police officers.

The Guardian, another British paper, reported that News International had settled cases brought by several people who had threatened to sue for having their phones hacked. James Murdoch, who had been running BSkyB when the alleged phone-hacking took place but was subsequently put in charge of the newspaper business, approved some payments. He said on July 7 that he was not fully aware of the facts when he did so. That action could be probed by the public inquiry. So could the firm's persistent failure to clean house.

Other newspapers soon alleged that former The News of the World reporters had described widespread phone-hacking at the paper. News International reacted angrily. Rebekah Brooks, once editor of The News of the World and by then chief executive of News International, said The Guardian had "substantially and likely deliberately misled the British public".

## Notes

deride：取笑，嘲笑
colossus：巨人，大企业
partisan：党羽，帮伙
high-profile：高调的
public inquiry：听证会

## 默多克众叛亲离？

两周前，新闻集团还是默多克领导下的业内神话，摩拳擦掌欲成就史上最大收购案。现在收购就不用提了,鲁伯特·默多克也沦为笑柄。英国三大政党联手英国圣公会,其他媒体及众多名流齐齐对抗新闻集团。一位昔日叱咤风云的巨头立即成为众矢之的,在嘘声中退场。

英国报纸《世界新闻报》涉嫌贿赂警察谋取信息,非法窃听一些名人及**惨案受害者**的语音信箱遭到指控。其母公司新闻集团因此名声受损,**负面影响**已然浮出水面,而对英国政坛和媒体行为自由的影响未来会慢慢显现出来。

其实报纸并不是新闻集团的核心业务所在。与9年前同期相比,当时**报纸利润**占集团利润超过30%,反观2010年上半年仅13%。其英国分支机构新闻国际的收入不过杯水车薪。经营《世界新闻报》和《太阳报》的子公司收益也大幅度下降。《泰晤士报》和《星期日泰晤士报》均在亏损中。

但是报纸对默多克本人意义非凡。新闻集团的主管们谈起老板执迷于新闻选材时,有些不解,也有些无可奈何,默多克甚至对内容排版都要亲自过问。这些报纸扩大了默多克在英国的政治影响力。大多数英国报纸都有各自倾向的党派。新闻国际发行的报纸左右许多政治立场不坚定的读者。

假设此次"窃听门"影响只限于英国报纸或者只是有关默多克的声誉和政治影响力,那么天大的事也能搞定,怕只怕好戏还在后头。警方调查和公开听证一触即发。新闻集团的领导层和继任者悬而未决,目前看来大变动确定无疑。英国天空广播公司投标案胎死腹中,集团转型之举的如意算盘就此落空。新闻集团无法再按原计划行事,领导层也未必是其期望的。

本周,一名抗议者戴着默多克头像面具,身穿罪犯服装出现在这位报业巨子伦敦的家门口。当然,默多克本人不会锒铛入狱,但是其他人就很难说了。日前,英国警方正对电话窃听和贿赂指控进行调查。7月12日警方向议会报告称,从《世界新闻报》前私人侦探格伦·穆尔凯尔那里搜缴来的文件看,有近4000人位于被窃听名单,目前警方已经通知了其中的170人。穆尔凯尔所做的惊人之举中的一小部分就已经足以对新闻集团提起**刑事诉讼**和民事诉讼。根据《英国调查权利管理法案》,如果有证据表明公司管理层"同意或默许"如窃听之类的犯罪行为,则涉案公司就有可能被判有罪。

美国政客对恐怖袭击受害人成为电话窃听目标一事表示愤怒不已,并呼吁介入调查。有人建议美国司法部根据《反海外贿赂法》对此事进行调查,该法案广泛适用于打击世界各地发生的贿赂。但是律师丹佛斯·纽科姆指出,该法案主要适用于"获得或维持"生意的贿赂,对于是否贿赂警察以获取信息的行为该法案规定尚不明确。美国人暂不出手的另一原因是英国向来在反腐败司法处理上表现地很出色。英国新的《反贿赂法》已于7月1日生效。

对电话窃听事件进行司法调查同样会产生诸多不良后果。高调的公开调查会产生超过其应有的影响,有关人员可能会因此辞职。此次调查似乎表明,新闻国际和新闻集团都对《世界新闻报》的不法行为缺乏足够的调查。该报王牌编辑克莱夫·古德曼和私家侦探穆尔·凯尔被定罪之后,新闻国际于2007年曾对其内部邮件进行了调查。随后公司高管报告议会称他们没有找到电话窃听的广泛证据。但是,现在看来,公司这些邮件中显然含有向警察贿赂的证据。

据另一份英国报纸《卫报》报道,许多人都曾扬言要因电话被窃听而起诉新闻国际,但新闻国际最终还是摆平了他们。窃听事件发生之时,詹姆斯·默多克正在经营英国天空电视台,之后他接管了《世界新闻报》,同时批准了对这些欲上诉者的赔偿。7月7日的时候他声称自己并没有完全了解事实的真相。公众听证会将会对此事进行调查。同时也会对该公司在内部管理上的长期失职进行问责。

其他报纸也很快报道了此事,称《世界新闻报》的前记者曾透露这家报纸存在着大量窃听事件。新闻国际对此给予了愤怒回应。当时的新闻国际负责人、《世界新闻报》前编辑丽贝卡·布鲁克说《卫报》"严重而且似乎是故意误导了英国民众"。

观察 OBSERVATION

**More to Read**

在默多克集团的窃听风波中,我们可以看到事件背后被揭开的黑幕,也可以看到遭窃听的受伤者。其中,既有基于善良的出发点,也有纯粹为制造公众效应的恶作剧心态,新闻媒体在完成引导公众趣味的任务后,渐渐开始向迎合观众口味的反方向退化,这不得不说是一种悲哀。全世界范围内,各媒体在竞争下出尽手段寻求"独家新闻",出格举动已是数不胜数。默多克的窃听风波揭开了一个盖子,逼迫以"监督"为诉求的新闻机构不得不反躬自省。

## Reading Guidance

2008年美国总统大选中,奥巴马以365足够多的选举票数压倒麦凯恩,成功当选美国第56届总统,也成为美国历史上首位黑人总统。奥巴马胜选的历史意义不仅仅在于他的肤色,更多地在于他真切地向世人演绎了一个"美国梦"。当选期间,奥巴马面对停滞不前的经济,为了创造更多的就业机会,推出了经济刺激计划。为兑现他总统竞选中的诺言,公布了新医疗改革方案;此外,新能源方案、新教育方案也相继出台。当然,这些方案的实施,既会给美国带来福音,同时也可能带来不安,这都将影响到他是否能够连任,续写美国传奇。

## Barack Obama:
## Can Anybody Beat Him?

Some say it was the bullet to Osama bin Laden's head. Others point to the Republicans' seemingly insatiable desire to inflict self-harm since they took back control of the lower house of Congress in last year's elections. And then there is the growing realization that Barack Obama might just have saved America from economic disaster.

Whatever the cause, a president who just a few weeks ago was regarded by his political opponents as being on the ropes before the fight for re-election had even properly begun is now being treated with a new, grudging respect as his poll numbers rise and he comes out punching.

Earlier this year, even those who argued that Obama was still favored for re-election in 18 months were forced to concede that he was being dragged down by a host of problems.

His popularity ratings plummeted as many independent voters shied away from a president they regarded as too ideological on issues such as healthcare reform and not focused enough on economic revival or cutting the deficit. The drumbeat of rightwing radio and Fox News constantly questioned the president's legitimacy and painted him as somehow un-American. Even among many of Obama's supporters there was disillusionment at what they saw as his disinclination to stand up for what he, and they, believed in. He was too cowed by criticism from the right, they said; too willing to seek a consensus that amounted to surrender.

In November, the Republicans seized control of the House of Representatives, greatly reduced the Democratic party's majority in the Senate, and declared the victory as a repudiation of all that Obama stood for. It was a stunning reversal for a man who had won an election just two years earlier with a message of hope that seemed to have buried a disheartened and divided Republican party.

But in recent weeks Obama's approval ratings have risen significantly—to a 16-month high of 53% in the most recent poll—and the president is widely thought to have rediscovered some of his old political mojo in the wake of the raid to kill Bin Laden. Meanwhile, Obama's crowd-pleasing tour of Ireland and Britain did him no harm back home.

For many pundits, that recent run of success was making the president look like a certainty for re-election. But then on Thursday, the well was poisoned by a single statistic: that U.S. economic growth had slumped to an annualized rate of just 1.8% in the first quarter of this year.

"That's miserable," said Larry Sabato, head of the University of Virginia's Centre for Politics, who has made a specialty of studying the factors that influence presidential elections. "There's probably only one thing that can beat Obama. You never know about scandal, but I doubt it. War and peace: we don't have Iraq now and Afghanistan's winding down. But the economy—I don't care how good a president he looks a year and a half out, if you have a growth rate that is well below 3%, that president is probably going to lose as long as the opposition party nominates a respectable candidate."

Obama has most to fear from a moderate Republican candidate. Three stand out among those likely to run: Mitt Romney, the former Massachusetts governor; Tim Pawlenty, the former Minnesota governor, and Jon Huntsman, the former US ambassador to China and ex-governor of Utah. All are former state governors, who often make compelling candidates—think of Bill Clinton, a former governor of Arkansas—because they are used to winning and using power by reaching across the political divide

In a Gallup poll released on Thursday, Huntsman fared the worst of the three Republican contenders thought most likely to be able to bring down Obama. He pulled in just 2% of support among likely Republican primary voters. Romney leads the field with 17%; Sarah Palin sits just a couple of points behind.

Romney has moved further to the right as his aspirations have grown but he has enough crossover appeal to be palatable to many independents. Tea Partiers and small-government activists, however, do not like it that, as governor, he signed legislation that provided near-universal healthcare insurance for Massachusetts residents—not least because health reform is now a favorite conservative stick with which to beat Obama.

But if the Republican right can forgive Romney such ideological transgressions, those same issues could prove powerful in luring the independents and conservative Democrat voters who are unhappy with Obama's first term.

Not so with Palin. Palin's recent purchase of a house in Arizona and the recruiting of an expanded staff has intensified speculation that she is about to enter the race. Her star has fallen considerably since it shone so brightly over the Republican landscape three years ago. Some of her erstwhile supporters have grown weary of her political missteps, such as her ill-judged defence of gun-toting rhetoric after the shooting of Arizona congresswoman Gabrielle Giffords in January. Others have been driven away by Palin's vague blandishments when it comes to policy specifics on issues that matter.

The battle over government spending will provide the backdrop to the next 18 months of campaigning by both parties as the Republicans wrestle with just how far to push back against Obama's economic stimulus plans and how deep to cut.

## Notes

plummet: 笔直落下

Gallup poll: 盖洛普民意调查, 被各大媒体认为是代表民意的一项权威调查, 具有普遍影响力。

Tea party: Taxed Enough Already。茶叶党, "暴怒的美国人联盟", 对奥巴马政府不满的一股政治势力。

erstwhile: 从前的, 往昔的

# 美国总统大选,奥巴马无人能敌?

一些人认为击毙本·拉登为奥巴马在下一届总统大选中增加了政治筹码,一些人则将矛头指向共和党,认为是他们自从在去年的选举中拿回了众议院的控制权后变得贪得无厌而导致自食恶果的下场。然而,现在人们愈发认识到,奥巴马仅仅是把美国从经济危机中解救出来而已。

无论做出何种解释,这位总统现在因民调支持率上升正受到新的礼遇,尽管这种礼遇颇有勉强意味。与此同时,他已着手反击。然而仅仅在几星期前,甚至改选之战尚未拉开帷幕之时,这位总统一度被政敌认为连任无望。

今年早些时候,那些认为在未来18个月之中奥巴马仍然是改选热门的人们也不得不承认,一系列问题一直在阻碍他的竞选之路。

此前,奥巴马的民调支持率骤降。这是因为许多独立选民认为,这位总统在诸如医保改革等问题上的做法过于理想化,而在经济复苏或削减赤字方面又未全力以赴,因此对他敬而远之。而右翼电台和福克斯新闻网不断质疑其总统的合法性,把他大肆渲染成"非美国人"。甚至许多奥巴马的支持者对他不愿意坚持自己和他们的信仰而大失所望。他们说,面对右翼团体的批评,他显得太过怯懦,而寻求政见统一无异于屈服。

11月,共和党重新掌控众议院,同时削弱民主党在参议院的大部分成员,与此同时,共和党将此次胜利宣称是对奥巴马政府的否定。这对于两年前刚刚赢得总统大选的奥巴马来说无疑是一次惊天大逆转。奥巴马为人们传递出的希望似乎结束了不得人心且内部分歧严重的共和党。

但是最近几周奥巴马的民意支持率显著提高,在最近的民意调查中达

## 观察 OBSERVATION

到了16个月来的新高——53%。此外,人民普遍认为,奥巴马在击毙本·拉登的行动后,政治上重新受到偏爱。此外,奥巴马对爱尔兰、英国的访问也进展得十分愉快,取得了良好的效果。

在许多权威人士看来,最近一系列的成功似乎预示着这位总统在重新选举中胜利在望。然而,出其不意的是,大好形势却因一项统计数字变得扑朔迷离。数字显示美国的经济增长率在今年的第一季度大幅度下降,年增长率仅为1.8%。

美国弗吉尼亚大学政治中心的主席拉里·萨巴图开设了一门专业,专门研究影响总统选举的因素。他说道:"这太糟糕了,可能只有一件事情可以击败奥巴马。你们可能对于丑闻一无所知,但是我对此却持怀疑态度。从战争和和平角度而言,我们现在没有伊拉克战争的困扰,阿富汗的局势也渐渐稳定下来。但是,从经济角度而言,我不关心总统如何看待这一年半以来的经济形势,但是经济增长率若低于3%,那么只要反对党提名一个合适的候选人,奥巴马总统很有可能会在选举中失败。"

奥巴马总统也不得不担心来自共和党候选人的威胁。三位候选人可能成为他的主要竞争对手。米特·罗姆尼,马萨诸塞州前州长;蒂姆·普兰提,明尼苏达州前州长;以及美国前驻华大使、犹他州前州长洪博培。这三位此前都担任过州长职位。从阿肯色州前州长比尔·克林顿的经历可以看出,他们将成为强有力的总统候选人,因为他们善于越过政治分歧获取和运用权力。

盖洛普组织星期四发布了民意调查,该调查显示,在三个最有可能击败奥巴马总统的共和党候选人中,洪博培的民众支持率最低,仅仅获得了2%的支持率;米特·罗姆尼在共和党候选人当中遥遥领先,获得17%的支持率;萨拉·佩林紧随其后,仅仅落后几个百分点。

随着野心的不断膨胀,米特·罗姆尼在政治态度上渐渐向右派靠拢。但是,这并不妨碍他获得其他派别的青睐,例如他迎合众多的独立选民的诉求。一些"茶叶党"人士和小政府积极分子却对罗姆尼在担任马赛诸塞州州长期间签署立法,为马萨诸塞州民众提供了几乎覆盖全民的医疗保健新政策做法不予认同。他们反对并不是因为医疗改革这项举措是保守派们现在击败奥巴马总统的一项有利的工具。

　　然而，如果共和党成员们对罗姆尼思想上的背离表示可以理解的话，那么上面提及的问题会有力地为他争取到更多的对奥巴马在第一个任期内表现不满的独立选民和保守的民主党人士的支持。

　　对佩林来说，形势却不容乐观。最近她在亚利桑那州购买豪宅并积极扩大自己团队的政治规模，人们推测她有可能加入到竞选的行列。但是3年前她曾在共和党的大选中大放异彩之后，其受欢迎度就大大下降了。显然，她以前的支持者因她政治上的失误已经对她丧失信心。她在谈及今年1月发生的美国联邦众议员吉福兹遭枪击案时，主张随身携带枪支以自卫，这一主张显然是有欠思考的。此外，佩林在一些具体政策上也做出冠冕堂皇的回应，也使部分利益相关者对她远离三分。

　　由于共和党正在探讨在多大程度上抵制奥巴马的经济刺激计划以及如何削减政府支出，所以在接下来的18个月的竞选活动之中，关于政府财政支出的争论将会成为两党竞争的又一个焦点。

**More to Read**

　　美国的总统选举实质上是两个政党之间的利益之争，不管总统职位花落谁家，最终维护的都是政党的权益。2012年美国总统大选的帷幕已经拉开，谁将会与奥巴马争锋？从目前的共和党候选人来看，马萨诸塞州前州长米特·罗姆尼虽然票数落后，但其背后丰厚的资金支持与成功的商界经验仍使他被认为是总统选举共和党候选人的有力竞争者，全国调查显示他目前是共和党选民对党内总统候选人提名的首选。其他两位候选人也不甘落后，共和党三强鼎立的局面业已形成。同时也不排除悍将出马的机会。而他们争论的议题还是围绕经济形势和社会福利等话题。目前竞争日益白热化，各个党派也使出了杀手锏，到底谁会登上总统宝座？我们拭目以待。

## Reading Guidance

美国最大的网络电子商务公司——亚马逊公司是一家进入财富500强的企业，总部位于美国华盛顿州的西雅图。亚马逊是网络上最早开始经营电子商务的公司之一，成立于1995年，一开始只经营网络的书籍销售业务，现在则扩及了范围相当广的其他产品，包括了影视光碟、音乐光碟、电脑、软件、电视游戏、电子产品、衣服、家具等等。本文借亚马逊公司推出最新平板电脑"烈火"之际，探讨亚马逊的营销策略，并将其与美国苹果公司和巴诺公司产品进行比较，从而凸显其价格优势。

# Amazon: The Walmart of the Web

A couple of years after it launched its website in 1995, Amazon was the subject of an unflattering report entitled "*Amazon Toast*". The pundit who penned it predicted that the fledgling online bookseller would soon be crushed by Barnes & Noble (B&N), a book-retailing behemoth which had just launched its own site.

Far from being crushed, Amazon is doing the crushing. Borders, a once-mighty book chain, was flattened this year. B&N looks like a frightened capy-

bara running from a fierce Brazilian she-warrior. Amazon is now one of the web's most successful e-tailers. Even Apple is feeling the heat.

On September 28 Jeff Bezos, Amazon's boss, unveiled a tablet computer called the Kindle Fire. It will compete with gadgets such as B&N's Nook Color tablet and Apple's iPad. The new Amazon tablet, which has a somewhat smaller screen than the iPad and only offers Wi-Fi connectivity, is likely to be just the first salvo in a titanic battle.

Like Apple, Amazon boasts a huge collection of online content, including e-books, films and music. And like Apple, it lets people store their content in a computing "cloud" and retrieve it from almost anywhere. But the two firms part company when it comes to pricing. The Kindle Fire, which will be available from mid-November in America, will cost only $199. That is far less than the cheapest iPad, a Wi-Fi-only device which costs $499. B&N responded to the Kindle Fire by cutting the price of its Nook Color to $224. This week Amazon also rolled out a new range of Kindle e-readers, the cheapest of which costs just $79. "We are building premium products and offering them at non-premium prices," beamed Mr. Bezos.

Amazon's decision to undercut its rivals is partly a tactic designed to disrupt the tablet market, which is still dominated by the iPad. Gartner, a research firm, reckons that Apple's device will account for almost three-quarters of the 64m tablets it thinks will be sold worldwide this year. Amazon's pricing strategy also reflects one of the firm's core beliefs, which is that cheap stuff makes customers cheerful. Call it the Walmart of the web.

Low prices are not the only thing underpinning Amazon's success. The company is technologically adept, and it has a knack of delighting customers with innovations such as its $79-a-year "Amazon Prime" shopping service in America, which offers members free, two-day shipping and other benefits. Such goodies have been crucial to its growth. But its ability to drive down the prices of everything from cameras to cloud computing gives it a colossal competi-

## 观 察 OBSERVATION

tive advantage.

A recent study by William Blair, an investment bank, underlines the price gap between Amazon and its rivals in the retailing world. The report compared the prices of 100 randomly selected goods at each of 24 American retailers with those items that were also available on Amazon.com. It found that almost half of the goods were listed on the online retailer's site too, and that Amazon's prices for individual products were on average 11% below those of the stores. The study also noted that Amazon's discounts were in many cases deeper than those offered by the retailers' own websites.

Admittedly, as an online outfit Amazon does not pay sales tax in American states where it has no physical presence. Many cash-strapped states are now keen to pass laws that would change this—a move Amazon is loudly and unsurprisingly opposing. But the William Blair study concludes that even if it has to cough up more tax, Amazon will still be able to offer prices that are lower than many rivals'. The firm's huge scale and its massively popular website, which it will use to promote the Kindle Fire, give it an edge. And it enjoys another advantage too. "Amazon does not have to worry about the impact of its pricing on a legacy store system," explains Kirthi Kalyanam, a professor at Santa Clara University's Retail Management Institute.

Amazon Web Services (AWS), which rents computing capacity in its giant data centers to customers, has also won a reputation for being cheap. Comparing cloud-computing prices is tricky, but observers of the market report that AWS is typically one of the lowest-cost providers. "Amazon operates with economies of scale that are practically impossible to match," says Reuven Cohen of Enomaly, which runs SpotCloud, an online marketplace where firms sell excess cloud-computing capacity.

The cloud is crucial to the success of Amazon's gadget strategy. Most analysts think that the firm loses money on the hardware that it sells. But it hopes that its cheap tablet will be wildly popular and therefore boost sales of Amazon's

cloud-based content, just as the Kindle e-reader boosted sales of e-books. It's like free parking outside Walmart—you want potential customers to see what's in the window.

The good news for Amazon is that tablet users seem more inclined to splash out on stuff than web shoppers who use PCs, according to Forrester, another research firm. One possible explanation for this is that tablet buyers tend to be richer; another is that the immersive experience tablets create encourages more impulse buying.

Whatever the reason, Amazon will have to hope that its gambit works, because its business model has at least one worrying downside. Its profit margin is a page-thin 3%—4%, partly because it has invested so heavily in the cloud. Now it is going head-to-head with Apple, which made a juicy $7.3 billion net profit on revenues of $28.6 billion in the latest quarter. Apple may not want to provoke a price war in the tablet market, where it sees plenty of growth to come. But if it does return fire, Amazon could get its fingers toasted.

## Notes

Barnes & Noble(B&N): 巴诺书店,是美国最大的实体书店,同时销售电子产品、光碟、游戏软件等等,全美拥有将近800家店面,公司亦是全球第二大网上书店,仅次于第一名的亚马逊。

e-tailer: 网络零售商

underpinning: 基础,支柱,支撑

tricky: 狡猾的,诡计多端的

观 察 OBSERVATION

# 亚马逊：网上沃尔玛

亚马逊在1995年推出网站，短短几年之后亚马逊就受到一篇报道直言不讳的抨击，这篇报道名为《亚马逊牌烤面包》。执笔专家预测，这家羽翼未丰的网络图书零售商将很快被巴诺公司击败(B&N)，巴诺公司是图书零售巨头，那时刚推出其网站不久。

结果亚马逊没有被击垮，反而一举歼灭了对手。曾强大一时的连锁书店鲍德斯于今年早期被打倒。而巴诺公司看起来则像只受惊吓的水豚，正飞奔着逃离这位勇猛的巴西女战士。现在亚马逊俨然已成为最成功的网络零售商之一，连苹果对之也要忌惮三分。

2011年9月28日，亚马逊老板杰夫·贝索斯发布了一款平板电脑，"烈火"，此款电脑将成为巴诺公司Nook Color及苹果公司iPad的强劲对手。新款亚马逊平板电脑的触摸屏小于iPad并且只提供无线连接。很有可能的是此款平板电脑的推出将会打响激烈竞争之战的第一枪。

与苹果相似，亚马逊号称其拥有大量的在线内容，其中包括电子书、电影和音乐。在另一点与苹果相似，它允许人们将自己的内容存储在它的计算云中，并且可以从几乎任何地方检索到信息。但是，这两家公司在对产品的定价上却大相径庭。"烈火"11月中旬将在美国上市，仅售199美元。这比只有Wi-Fi功能售价为499美元，最便宜的iPad还要便宜得多。本周，亚马逊还将推出一系列新款电子阅读器，最便宜的仅售79美元。亚马逊的老板杰夫·贝索斯神采奕奕地说："我们打造优质的产品并以低价提供给消费者。"

亚马逊以低价策略削弱竞争对手，其主要用意是在于，打破苹果公司平板电脑iPad的垄断局面。高德纳研究公司认为,苹果的平板电脑将会占今年全球平板电脑总销量约75%的份额,预计今年全球范围内将售出为6400台。亚马逊的定价策略同时也反映出公司的一大核心理念,那就是"低价吸引客户",人称"网络沃尔玛"。

低价并不是唯一促成亚马逊成功的原因。该公司以技术著称,同时它还掌握了如何使用创新取悦顾客的诀窍,比如在美国79美元一年的"亚马逊优惠"购物服务,为会员提供"2天免费送达"服务及其他优惠。这些极具吸引力的好处对于亚马逊的发展极为关键。可是,亚马逊能够压低从照相机到云计算一切商品的价格,这样的能力使之拥有巨大的竞争优势。

投资银行的威廉·布莱尔最近的一项研究说明了亚马逊与其零售业对手之间的价格差距。该报告从24家美国零售商每一家中随机挑选出100件商品,这些商品在亚马逊的线上商店也有,并对比了两者的价格。报告发现,近乎一半的商品在亚马逊线上商店有,而且个人物品在亚马逊上的价格较之商店里平均低11%。根据该报告,在一些情况下,亚马逊的打折力度较之一些零售商的网店打折力度还要大。

诚然,作为一个在线供应商,亚马逊不必向美国的各州缴纳消费税,因为它并没有实体店。一些现金紧缺的州目前热衷于通过立法来改变这种现状,这一举动招致亚马逊毫不意外的强烈反对。但是威廉·布莱尔在其研究报告总结道,即便是亚马逊勉强同意缴纳更多的税赋,它依然能够提供比一些竞争者更低的价格。公司巨大的规模和其大受欢迎的网站会大力推广"烈火",这将是一个无可比拟的优势。同时,亚马逊还具备另一优势。圣塔克拉拉大学零售管理学院的教授克西·卡利亚纳姆说:"亚马逊不会担心对销售留存系统的定价所带来的影响。"

亚马逊网络服务系统将其庞大数据中心的计算能力出租给客户,赢得了物美价廉的声誉。相比之下,云计算的价格复杂多变,但是市场观察家们说,亚马逊网络服务系统是成本最低的供应商之一。Enomaly是一家正经营新型云计算经营模式的公司,该模式是在线市场供一些公司出售过剩的云计算能力,它的创始人鲁文·科恩说:"亚马逊经营形成的规模经济实际上无可比肩的。"

## 观察 OBSERVATION

云计算是亚马逊便携终端战略成功的关键所在。多数分析家认为该公司在其出售的硬件设备上遭受了损失。但是，亚马逊希望便宜的平板电脑能大受欢迎，并因此推动亚马逊基于云计算内容的销售，就像电子阅读器推动电子书的销售一样。这就如同沃尔玛商场外的免费泊车，你希望潜在的消费者看见橱窗里是些什么。

据福瑞斯特研究公司研究，对亚马逊来说一个好消息是，平板电脑用户在商品上是似乎比使用电脑的购物者更愿意一掷千金。有可能解释这一现象的是，平板电脑的购买者趋于更加富有；另一个解释是，平板电脑带来沉浸式的体验鼓励了更多的冲动消费。

不论是什么原因，亚马逊都希望其策略奏效，因为它的商业模式存在至少一个隐患。其利润空间只有薄如纸张的3%-4%，部分原因是亚马逊在云计算上投资过多。现在，它开始与苹果针锋相对，苹果从去上季度286亿美元的收入中获取了73亿美元的净利润。苹果可能不愿在平板电脑市场掀起价格大战，它在这一市场中看到了巨大的利润增长空间。但是，如果苹果反击，那么亚马逊可能会焦头烂额。

**More to Read**

　　有人认为能与苹果叫板的也许只有亚马逊了。现在的亚马逊是放弃了"赚硬件一次的钱"来博得"赚内容上一辈子的钱"的入场券。因为硬件只销售一次，而内容消费却是"一辈子的钱"，而"烈火"的横空出世让亚马逊的股价逆市上涨了2.4%也恰恰证明了这一点。其竞争对手美国最大的连锁实体书店巴恩斯·诺布尔公司的股价则大跌6.8%。苹果的股价也下跌了0.59%。贝索斯冒着拉低公司利润率的巨大风险在强推"烈火"，显然没有给自己留后路。这一重拳出击能否取得成功关键还是要看市场的认可度。尽管价格是能否成功的一个关键因素，但是市场分析师依然认为，"烈火"不足以向iPad发起挑战。到底霸主地位花落谁家，我们尚不能早早地下结论，但时间会给我们最终的答案。

Reading Guidance

受非洲持续大旱的影响,索马里饥荒不断加剧,联合国称将对数百万难民进行紧急人道主义援助。世界粮食计划署、联合国难民总署、联合国粮农署等国际组织纷纷发表声明对索马里提供救援。本文作者卡云勒卡亚,是无国界医生组织的(MSF)新任主席。他出生于印度喀拉拉邦,是无国界医生首位亚裔国际议会主席,曾在非洲参与过多次救援活动。本文是索马里发生灾荒时他写的一篇报告,报告中描述了索马里区域内的灾情,指出这场饥荒是天灾,更是人祸。通过本文对索马里饥荒的透析,我们应更多地反思一下,并树立正确的人道主义观。

## Famine in Somalia: A Man-made Crisis

The emergency unfolding in and around Somalia is being portrayed by many aid organizations and the media in one-dimensional terms, such as "famine in the Horn of Africa" or "worst drought in 60 years". But only blaming natural causes ignores the complex geopolitical realities exacerbating the situation and suggests that the solution lies in merely finding funds and shipping enough food. Glossing over the man-made causes of hunger and starvation in the

观 察 OBSERVATION

region and the difficulties in addressing them will not help resolve the crisis.

I have just returned from Kenya and Somalia and what I and my Médecins Sans Frontières (MSF) colleagues are seeing indicates a profoundly distressing situation. In Mogadishu, I met a young woman from the southern region of Lower Shebelle who is now living in one of the many makeshift camps appearing all over the city. She left home with her husband and seven children because of a bad harvest and her inability to afford food and water. Somewhere along her trek, she had to leave her husband and three children behind, as they were too weak to complete the five-day walk.

Her story echoes those of thousands of other families in southern and central Somalia who have been ravaged by conflict for years and were tipped over the edge by drought. Malnutrition is chronic in many parts of the Horn of Africa and there needs to be a long-term international effort to ensure nutritious foods reach the people who need them. Today, however, the most urgent needs are concentrated in southern and central Somalia. Even if we do not have a full picture, we know the situation is dire from the large numbers of Somalis arriving in weak condition in the capital, Mogadishu, and at camps across the border in Kenya and Ethiopia.

The failed harvests exacerbated what was already a catastrophe. Somalia is the theatre for a brutal war between the transitional government, backed by western nations and supported by African Union troops, and armed opposition groups, most notably al-Shabaab. It is this war, combined with the internecine rivalries of the various Somali clans, that has kept independent international assistance away from many communities. The Somali people are trapped between various forces trying to weaken their opponents. There is virtually no access to healthcare in vast tracts of land across the country.

Against this backdrop, it is difficult for medical humanitarian organizations to expand health services and have an impact. MSF has been working in Somalia for two decades and has projects in nine locations on both sides of the front-

lines. We already have more than 8000 acutely malnourished children in our feeding programs. But all four of the children I met who made it from Lower Shebelle have measles in addition to malnutrition. They live with thousands of other displaced people in crowded, unsanitary conditions. Others from these camps complain of skin and eye infections, watery diarrhea and respiratory tract infections. Some are too weak even to seek food or healthcare.

Scaling up operations inside Somalia is slow, and we are constantly being forced to make tough choices. Without the ability to carry out independent assessments and provide assistance in what we believe to be the hardest-hit areas, we will not be able to prevent the worst consequences of this emergency.

Humanitarian aid has come to be seen by all sides in the conflict as either an opportunity or a threat. Al-Shabaab has placed bans on foreign staff, on the supply of medicines and materials by air, and on vaccination activities. Elsewhere, seemingly simple procedures like hiring a nurse or renting a car can turn into endless negotiations when a rapid response is needed.

Providing aid in Somalia today is about as grim as it gets. Our staff is at constant risk of being shot or abducted. And we may never be able to reach the communities most in need of help, or have to compromise some of our independence when we do reach them.

Impressive amounts of money for food and other supplies are being raised and sent to the region. But MSF warns that the crisis requires more than raising cash alone, noting that drought is exacerbated by Somalia's "failed political landscape" where warring forces block aid to weaken opponents.

Now, the United Nations is appealing for three hundred million dollars in the next two months. Officials say much of that will be used to supply existing feeding centers and to provide medical services. The money will also be used to support local economies and farmers. "The only way to prevent people moving out is to make sure that they have hope for the future—they can make something out of their lives. How can they do that? They can do that only if they feel that in the next few months they will be in condition to produce their food."

But I am concerned with the last mile: getting assistance and supplies from the ports of Mogadishu to the people who need it urgently.

## Notes

famine：饥荒
internecine：相互残杀的,两败俱伤的
backdrop：背景
humanitarian：人道主义的
exacerbate：使恶化,使加重

# 人造危机：索马里饥荒

许多救援组织和媒体在报道索马里及其周边地区发生的灾情时往往很片面,谓之"非洲之角大饥荒"或是"60年不遇的旱灾"。但是单纯把这一切都归咎于自然因素,会忽略了复杂的地缘政治现实,正是这一现实在加剧灾情,而且这种单纯指责自然因素的态度势必将解决方案局限于寻找救助资金和运送足够的食物。回避导致该地区饥荒的人为因素以及对处理这些人为因素时所遇到的困难避而不谈,对解决危情毫无助益。

我刚从肯尼亚和索马里回来。在那里,我和无国界医生组织(MSF)的同事们看到的是让人痛心的场面。我在摩加迪沙遇见一个来自下谢贝利南部的妇女,她住在临时难民营中,这种难民营在摩加迪沙随处可见。因为收成不好,她负担不起食物和水,她和她丈夫还有3个孩子只有逃离家

乡，另寻出路。在艰苦跋涉的途中，她的丈夫和孩子因身体过于虚弱而倒下了，她终于撑到了难民营。

索马里南部和中部千千万万的家庭经历着与这位妇女同样的遭遇，多年以来他们饱受地区冲突之苦，旱灾又使他们的生活雪上加霜。在非洲之角的许多地方，营养不良是长期的问题。确保营养充足的食物送到有需要的人手上，需要国际社会的不懈努力。然而，如今有最迫切需要的地方集中在索马里的中部和南部。即使我们还没有全面的信息，但从抵达首都城市摩加迪沙以及跨越边境抵达肯尼亚与埃塞俄比亚营地的大批索马里人的虚弱情况看来，我们可知情况是何其严峻。

收成不好，令这场灾难恶化。索马里是一场残酷战争的舞台，参战其中一方是得到西方国家作为强大后盾，并获非洲联盟军队支持的过渡政府，另一方则是以青年党为主的武装反对组织。就是这场战事，再加上多个索马里敌对部落之间的互相残害，令很多社区无法获得独立的国际援助。索马里人被困于不同的派系斗争之中，在这个土地辽阔的国家之中，人民实际上没有可以得到医疗护理的途径。

在此背景下，人道主义医疗救援组织就很难实施医疗救助服务，也无法发挥作用。无国界医生组织（MSF）在索马里地区已经工作20余载。在交战双方前线（即过渡联邦政府以及青年党的控制地区）的9个地点设有救援项目。其中的营养治疗项目已经接收了8000多名急性营养不良儿童，我见到的4名由下谢贝利州前来的孩子，除了营养不良之外还染上麻疹。他们与数以千计的流离失所者，一起居住在挤迫和不卫生的环境中。在这些营地的其他人，皮肤和眼睛也受到感染，出现水样腹泻和呼吸道感染。一些人更是虚弱得无法进食或接受医疗护理。

在索马里扩大救援行动是缓慢而艰辛的。在展开或扩大救援工作时，无国界医生业经常被迫做出艰难抉择。若无法做出独立的评估、无法在我们认为是最受影响的地区提供援助，我们将不能在这场紧急情况中，阻止最坏的结果发生。

参与冲突的各方将人道救援看成一个机会，或者威胁。青年党已经对外籍救援人员下了禁令，并禁止空运的药物和物资进入，以及禁止进行疫

## 观察 OBSERVATION

苗注射项目。此外,聘请护士或租车这种看似简单的程序,也可能要花上大量的宝贵时间进行无休止协商,从而阻碍做出快速决定。

今日,在索马里提供救援的现实情况愈演愈烈。我们的工作人员时常冒着遭受射击或绑架的风险。就是我们可能永远无法向最有需要的社群伸出援手,又或者当我们协助他们时,我们的独立性也得做出一些妥协。

现在正在募集捐款,以购买食物和其他物资,运送到这个地区。但是无国界医生组织(MSF)警示说仅仅筹集资金是不够的,指出索马里"失败的政治局面"是加剧灾情的主要原因,相互敌对的双方封锁外部援助为了达到削弱对方的目的。

目前,联合国正呼吁在未来两个月筹集3亿美元。官员们表示,其中大部分钱将用于维持现有的供养中心并提供医疗服务。这些钱还将用于支持当地经济和农民。"防止人们迁出的唯一途径是确保他们对未来抱有希望,即确保他们的生活有所成就。他们怎么才能实现这些呢?只有让他们觉得在未来几个月里,他们能够自己生产出食物。"

但我关注的是最后一个步骤,把援助和物资由摩加迪沙的港口,送到有迫切需要的人手上。

**More to Read**

英国前首相布莱尔曾说:"非洲是世界良心上的一块伤疤。"而如今,索马里饥荒或许是这块"伤疤"中最触目惊心的部分。联合国负责人道救援事务的助理秘书长凯瑟琳·布拉格说,索马里危机已成为"当今世界最严重的人道主义危机"。在造成索马里灾荒的原因中,我们看到有天灾,更有人祸。在我们人类居住的这个蓝色星球上,"阳光灼热之洲"是一片不可分割的美丽大陆,如何援助处于水深火热的非洲同胞也正考验着国际社会的"良心",一切要看我们如何回答。

## Reading Guidance

众所周知,美国是最早登上月球的国家。1969年,"阿波罗11号"载人飞船成功登月,标志着美国在同苏联的太空竞赛中取得决定性胜利。这一成就距美国总统肯尼迪发表著名的登月讲话,宣称要"在10年内把人类送上月球"仅相隔8年。现在看来,作为至今仍是唯一一个实现载人登月的国家,美国的太空优势也相当明显。美国的这一载人登月工程在世界航天史上也具有划时代意义。自从布什政府以来,美国一直酝酿再一次的登月计划,近日据美国媒体消息称,奥巴马政府已经彻底否决"重返月球"计划。但这并不意味着人们这一梦想的停止,相反,却掀起了私有公司竞争登月的狂潮。

## Race to the Moon for Private Firms

Now that the last space shuttle has landed back on Earth, a new generation of space entrepreneurs would like to whip up excitement about the prospect of returning to the Moon.

Spurred by a $30 million purse put up by Google, 29 teams have signed up for a competition to become the first private venture to land on the Moon.

Most of them are unlikely to overcome the financial and technical challenges to meet the contest deadline of December 2015, but several teams think they have a good shot to win—and to take an early lead in a race to take commercial advantage of our celestial neighbor.

At the very least, a flotilla of unmanned spacecraft could be headed Moonward within the next few years, with goals that range from lofty to goofy.

One Silicon Valley venture, Moon Express, is positioning itself as a future Fedex for Moon deliveries: if you have something to send there, the company would like to take it. Moon Express was having a party on Thursday night to show off the flight capabilities of its lunar lander, based on technology it licensed from NASA, and "to begin the next era of the private commercial race to the Moon," as the invitation put it.

"In the near future, the Moon Express lunar Lander will be mining the Moon for precious resources that we need here on Earth," the invitation promised. "Years from now, we will all remember we were there."

Naveen Jain, an Internet billionaire and a founder of Moon Express, says the company will spend $70 million to $100 million to try to win the Google Lunar X Prize, but could recoup its investment on its first flight. He envisions selling exclusive broadcast rights for video from the Moon, as well as sponsorships, for companies to put their logos on the Lander, or, perhaps, a tie-in to reality television.

"Wouldn't it be nice if you could have a 'Moon Idol,' just like 'American Idol?'" suggested Mr. Jain. "You take the top 10 contestants and play their voices on the Moon, record it and see who sounds the best." There is no air on the Moon to transmit sound waves, but "you could play it through the dust and see what it sounds like when you play it right on the surface," Mr. Jain said. His point was that with cheap lunar transportation, there was no predicting what might catch people's fancies.

Another competitor, Astrobotic Technology, intends to sell berths on its lu-

nar lander to space agencies and scientific institutions, which would pay $820000 a pound to send up their experiments. The company, a spinoff from Carnegie Mellon University, is building a large craft—much bigger than Moon Express's—capable of carrying 240 pounds of payload (read: $200 million of cargo) and hopes to be ready to launch in December 2013.

"We can make a lot of money even if we do not win the prize," said David Gump, president of Astrobotic. "We will be making substantial profit on the first flight. Basically, we'll break even by selling a third of the payload."

The X Prize competitors might all be beaten by landers and rovers that China, Russia and India plan to send up over the next couple of years. But those fall more in the mold of traditional, government-built science probes.

While NASA had wanted to send astronauts back to the Moon, its program was canceled last year, a victim of budget cuts and shifting priorities. But it has awarded $500,000 each to Moon Express, Astrobotic and a third competitor, Rocket City Space Pioneers.

George Xenofos, manager of NASA's Innovative Lunar Demonstrations Data program, said he expected one or more teams to make it to the Moon. "It's definitely not the technical issues that are stopping them," he said.

The contestants' goals do not appear to face legal hurdles. The Outer Space Treaty of 1967, ratified by 100 nations, bars countries from claiming sovereignty over any part of the Moon, but does not prevent private companies from setting up shop. As for mining the Moon, it could fall under similar legal parameters as fishing in international waters.

Although some orbiting spacecraft have crashed into the Moon in recent years, 35 years have passed since anything from Earth made a soft landing there. To some people, this looks like an overdue invitation.

"It's probably the biggest wealth creation opportunity in modern history," said Barney Pell, a former NASA computer scientist turned entrepreneur and now a co-founder of Moon Express. While Moon Express might initially make money by sending small payloads, the big fortune would come from bringing back platinum and other rare metals, Dr. Pell said. "Long term, the market is massive, no doubt," he said. "This is not a question of if. It's a question of who and when. We hope it's us and soon."

For the Moon competition, Google put up ＄30 million. Of that, ＄20 million will go to the first team to land a spacecraft on the Moon, explore 500 meters and send back high-definition video and photos. The second team will win ＄5 million, and the remaining ＄5 million will pay for bonus prizes like surviving a frigid lunar night or traveling more than 5000 meters on the surface.

## Notes

celestial：天空的
goofy：愚笨的
sponsorship：资助者的地位、任务等
sovereignty：最高统治权，国家的主权

# 私有公司登月竞赛

既然航天飞机时代已经随着最后一次飞行结束而落幕，新一代的航天企业家希望燃起人们重返月球的激情。

受到谷歌设立的3000万美元奖金的激励，29支团队已经报名参赛，竞逐第一支登陆月球的私人探险队这一殊荣。虽然他们之中的大多数不太可能在竞赛结束的2015年12月克服资金困难和技术瓶颈，但是，有几支

团队认为他们胜券在握,并能在月球商业开发的竞赛中拔得头筹。

至少,在几年之内,不管是出于科研或者是商业目的,几艘小型无人航天器可能会飞往月球。

一家位于硅谷的风险投资公司——月球快车,把自己定位为未来月球快递业的联邦快递:如果您有东西寄往月球,月球快车乐于为您服务。周四晚上该公司举办了一场派对,以展示其基于国家航空和宇宙航行局授权使用科技研发的月球登陆车的航行能力,并如邀请函所说,"展开私人登月商业竞赛的新纪元。"

"在不久的将来,月球快车登月飞行器可能会在月球上开采我们现在需要的资源。"邀请函中提到,"未来几年,我们都会记得曾经到达过月球。"

因特网巨富、月球快车的创始人纳威·简称,公司将投资7000万到1亿去努力争取谷歌设立的奖金,并称第一次登月飞行会将成本回收。他构想将从月球上拍摄视频的独家播放权进行竞拍,同时许诺赞助的公司,允许他们将自己公司的标志张贴在月球登陆器上。或者可以试图和美国的真人秀节目建立商业关系。

"如果我们有个像'美国偶像'一样的'月球偶像'不是很好吗?"简建议说,"我们选中前十名竞赛者,让他们在月球上讲话并将声音录下来,然后试听一下,看看谁的声音最动听。"在月球上没有空气传播声波,但是"你可以通过灰尘传播并且在地球表面试听录音效果",简说道。他的意图在于随着月球登陆费用的降低,没有什么是不可能预测的,这样就会满足大众渴望实现奇思异想的心理。

另一位竞争者,探月队科技公司也有意将月球登陆器上的座位出售给航天局和科研机构,登月飞行上平均每磅负载将价值82万美元。卡耐基梅隆大学附属的一家公司,正致力于建造一艘大型太空船,相比月球快车要大得多,能够负载240磅(相当于2亿美元的货物),有望在2013年12月实现登月计划。

即使我们没有赢得谷歌设立的奖金,我们也能赚很多的钱,探月队总裁大卫·邓普说道。"第一次的月球飞行可以为我们带来巨额利润。一般说来,我们卖掉酬载的三分之一就可以实现保本。"

奖金的追逐者很有可能会被中国、印度、俄罗斯的月球登陆器或巡游器打败。这些国家在未来两三年内有月球登陆计划，但是这些大部分是包含在传统的、政府支持的科研探索计划里。

尽管美国国家航空航天局此前计划向月球派遣宇航员，可是这一计划因经费削减和政策重心的调整在去年被迫取消。但是航空航天局分别奖励了月球快车、探月队和第三位竞争者城市空间火箭先行者50万美元。

美国国家航空航天局月球演示数据创新项目的负责人乔治·森诺福斯说，他期望有越来越多的队伍加入到登月竞赛中来。他说："妨碍他们加入的肯定不会是技术上的问题。"

竞赛者的目标并不在于去挑战法律的权威。1967年100个国家签署的《外层空间条约》明确规定禁止任何国家私自宣布占领月球某部分，但是并没有禁止私有公司在月球上设立站点。至于在月球上开采资源，可以参照在国际海域捕鱼的相关法律文件。

尽管部分在宇宙中运行的飞船在最近几年曾经闯入月球，但是自从那次来自地球的飞船在那里软着陆之后，35年过去了。这对于大多数人来说，更像是一次迟到的邀请。

企业家巴尼·派尔，以前是美国国家航空航天局的计算科学家，现在是月球快车的创始人之一。他认为这可能是现代历史上最好的致富机会。派尔说道，尽管月球快车最初可能只会通过出售部分载重来盈利，但是"大鱼"会出现在从月球带回铂和其他稀有金属之后。"从长期来看，市场潜力是巨大的。这一点毋庸置疑。这不是一个是否会盈利的问题，而是什么时间盈利，谁将会盈利的问题，我希望会是我们，而且是在不久的将来。"

这场登月竞赛，谷歌设立了3000万美元奖金。其中2000万将会奖励给第一支登月的队伍，这支队伍须探测500米同时发回月球的视频和图片。第二支队伍赢得500万，剩下的500万作为奖励，奖给那些在寒冷的月球过夜或者在月球表面飞行超过5000米的队伍。

**More to Read**

奥巴马政府宣布放弃"重返月球"计划后,引发了私有公司竞相登月的热潮。这在一定程度上折射出现在的美国经济和美国政府已经无力承担这一耗资巨大的登月计划,只能寄希望于私有企业的参与。究竟美国的私有企业能否不负所望,完成美国人民的这一梦想,我们还不能过早地下结论。但是,我们应当看出,这次登月竞赛已经被看做是财富创造的绝好机会,而并非单纯地实现美国在登月上的霸主地位。私有公司利用这次登月竞赛一方面大大提高了知名度,另一方面,如果竞赛成功的话,将会带来客观的收益,一举两得,何乐而不为呢?

观 察 OBSERVATION

**Reading Guidance**

　　爱情,这一亘古延绵的话题始终贯穿于人们的生活之中。爱情是"爱"和"情"的结合;爱是喜欢,爱是给予和奉献;情是两人之间的互相吸引和倾慕,是人与人之间的强烈依恋、亲近、向往,以及无私专一并且无所不尽其心的情感。爱情是人性的组成部分,是最美好的情感。如此美妙的情感是否会让陷入爱情的人们做出令人惊讶的举动呢? 科学研究说,当一个人陷入爱情,大脑中的12个区域会协同工作,释放出引发精神愉悦的化学物质,如多巴胺、催产素、肾上腺素和血压激素。如此多的激素就在西班牙第18任阿尔巴女公爵席尔瓦的身上作用了一把,据英国《卫报》8月7日报道,这位85岁高龄的"富姐儿"日前居然力抗子女甚至是西班牙国王的反对,愿意放弃财富,只为换取自由身下嫁一名比她年轻24年的小公务员。

# Money Really Can't Buy Love

　　Spain's fabulously rich Duchess of Alba has signed away her enormous wealth, string of palaces, priceless works of art and vast swathes of Spanish real estate to marry for love at 85.

　　The duchess—whose name is Maria Silva, is one of the richest women in

Spain. She is a distant relative of King James II, Winston Churchill and Diana, Princess of Wales and owns a dozen castles whose walls are hung with works by Goya, Velazquez and Rubens and huge stretches of land. Her wealth is estimated at between 600 million and 3.5 billion euros ($4.9 billion).

A fan of flamenco, bullfighting and all traditional Spanish celebrations, the Duchess of Alba, born in Madrid, according to Guinness World Records, has more titles than any noble on earth, in total of 46 titles—being a duchess seven times over, a countess 22 times and a marquesa 24. Hence, Spaniards joke if she meets up with England's Queen Elizabeth, it's the British queen who should curtsy to the duchess.

As head of the 539-year-old House of Alba, her privileges include not having to kneel before the Pope and the right to ride on horseback into Seville cathedral. But the children of the duchess, 85, have until now blocked her plans to marry Alfonso Diez, 24 years her junior.

The duchess and Diez, a civil servant in the department of social security who also runs a PR business. The duchess has divided her fortune between her six children to convince them that her suitor is besotted with her rather than her money and the kinds of possessions that are considered national treasures, reports said.

"Every great love story should end in marriage," the duchess told *Vanity Fair* magazine in May as she posed in the garden of one of her palaces, explaining why she wanted to make social security worker Alfonso Diez, 60, her third husband.

"I still don't know why my children are causing problems," the duchess complained to Spanish radio station La Cope in February.

Her six children who, as she likes to point out, are all divorced, were all borne from her first marriage to Pedro Luis Martinez de Irujoy Artazcoz, son of the Duke of Sotomayor, who died in 1972.

The duchess, who is rumoured to have undergone extensive cosmetic surgery, shocked the nation when in 1978 she remarried, this time to the priest Aguirre.

In 2008 it appeared that the proposed marriage to Diez had been called off when the House of Alba issued a statement saying that the relationship "was based on a long friendship and there are no plans to marry". The statement came after an alleged telephone call from King Juan Carlos discouraging the duchess from marrying Diez.

But whatever the king thinks it now appears the duchess is going ahead with the marriage, and the details have now emerged of how she plans to overcome her children's opposition: by giving them their inheritance in advance, even though Diez has signed a document renouncing any claim to her wealth.

"We aren't hurting anyone. If only things could be fixed... Alfonso doesn't want anything. All he wants is me," she said earlier this year.

According to a report, her eldest son Carlos inherits the Liria Palace in Madrid and the Monterrey Palace in Salamanca, as well as overall control of the family fortune. Much of the patrimony is managed by a foundation and, in return for tax breaks, belongs by law to the nation and cannot be sold.

"If in the end my mother decides to marry, we shall go, although we still don't agree," son Cayetano said in a recent interview.

## Notes

Pope: 教皇
inheritance: 遗产,继承物
renounce: 宣布放弃
tax break: 减税优惠

# 金钱买不了真爱

　　腰缠万贯的西班牙阿尔巴女公爵在85岁高龄之际,签字放弃巨额财富,包括多座宫殿、价值连城的艺术珍宝以及大片西班牙房产,只为嫁给心上人。

　　这位女公爵名为玛利亚席尔瓦,是西班牙最富有的女性之一,也是英国前首相丘吉尔和已故威尔士王妃黛安娜的远亲。女公爵的财产包括西班牙境内的宫殿和宅邸,委拉斯凯兹、戈雅、鲁本斯等名家画作以及大量地产,据估计资产总值在6亿至35亿欧元(约合49亿美元)之间。

　　她热爱弗拉明戈舞、斗牛以及所有的西班牙传统庆祝活动,根据吉尼斯世界纪录称,出生在马德里的阿尔巴女公爵一共有46个头衔,是世界上头衔最多的贵族,受封女公爵7次、女伯爵22次、女侯爵24次。因而西班牙人戏言,如果女公爵遇见英国的伊丽莎白女王,伊丽莎白女王也应该对公爵行屈膝礼。

　　身为有着539年历史的阿尔巴家族的掌门人,她的特权众多,包括不用在教皇面前下跪、可以骑马进入西班牙著名的塞维尔大教堂等。但是这位85岁女公爵的子女却企图阻止她嫁给年轻她24岁的阿方索·迭斯。

　　迭斯是西班牙社会保障部的公务员,同时拥有一家公关公司。女公爵为了说服子女们相信她的追求者爱的是她的人而不是她的钱或是所谓的国家财富而将财产分配给了自己的6个子女。

　　今年5月,她在自己一座宫殿的花园里接受《名利场》杂志采访时说:"每一段真爱最后都应走向婚姻。"解释了为什么她要选择60岁的社保工作者阿方索·迭斯做她第三任丈夫。

## 观察 OBSERVATION

2月份，女公爵向西班牙电台抱怨说，"我不明白我的孩子们为什么要惹麻烦。"

她的子女都是她和第一任丈夫索托马约尔公爵之子、工程师路易斯·马丁内斯·德·伊鲁霍所生，现在都是离异状态。女公爵的第一任丈夫在1972年就去世了。

路易斯去世后，有谣言称阿尔巴公爵做了一系列的整容手术，她在1978年嫁给神父阿奎尔，令许多西班牙人为之震惊。

席尔瓦和迭斯的婚讯最初于2008年传出，但就在据信西班牙国王胡安·卡洛斯致电她表示反对后，阿尔巴家族曾发表声明称"两人的关系是基于长期的友谊，并无结婚打算"。

然而，不论国王怎么想，女公爵已经要开始经营她的婚姻了，而且为了克服子女的反对，她已经将自己的家产提前分配给了子女，迭斯也签署声明宣布放弃继承阿尔巴的任何财产。

"我们没有伤害任何人。只要能结婚，阿方索什么都不要，他已经放弃一切。他只想和我在一起。"今年早些时候阿尔巴这样说道。

据报道，她的长子卡洛斯将继承坐落在马德里和萨拉曼卡的两座宫殿，并从总体上管理整个家族的财产。为了回报所享受的减税政策，大部分的祖产将由基金会管理，并通过法律属国家所有，不得出售。

在最近接受采访时，女公爵的儿子卡耶塔诺说："尽管我们始终不同意他们的结合，但是如果妈妈最终还是要结婚的话，我们会接受。"

**More to Read**

古今中外的婚姻历来讲究的是般配，那种门当户对、品貌相当的爱情总是让人艳羡不已。但是大千世界，无奇不有，随着社会的发展，人们道德观念的改变，越来越多的差距很大的爱情出现在我们的视线里。婚姻自由是爱情至高无上的准则，在这个大原则下，年龄和其他因素一样，并不能成为阻挡爱情的"绊脚石"。

## Reading Guidance

  2012年第三十届夏季奥林匹克运动会将在伦敦举行。伦敦是迄今为止举办夏季奥运会次数最多的城市，也是历史上首座三度举办奥运会的城市。针对奥运旅游，伦敦旅游局早已开始布局。以往，在重大比赛举行的当年内，通常人们会避免前往东道国及主办城市进行游览。这是由于很多人会先入为主地认为，比赛将会导致旅游景点物价飙升，也不容易找到住宿的酒店，但在2012年的英国是没有理由做这种猜测的——伦敦旅游局的口号是"像平时一样做生意"，英国旅游局和伦敦旅游局正在竭力消除潜在游客、媒体以及旅游公司对于价格和酒店的这些先入为主的担忧。伦敦——英国充满活力的魅力之都，2012的奥运盛会定会让它的旅游业发达一夏。

## London Olympics, Tourism or Not?

  London 2012 organizers last week published artists' impressions of how some of the yet-to-be-erected temporary facilities will look once the "greatest show on earth" hits town next year.

  Never mind the fact that British summers can be damp and drizzly—center court at Wimbledon has a roof for a good reason—and forget dire warnings of airport-style security and transport congestion.

The "overlay" vision, as organizers move into a new phase of the preparations with the "500 days to go" mark coming up next month, is strawberries and cream, picnics in the park, street parties and long, lazy summer evenings outdoors.

"We started this process two years ago and we looked at the festival nature of things," said John Barrow, a senior principal for architects and venue designers Populous.

"We looked at the Festival of Britain in 1951 and explored the delight in the innovation post-war… we also looked at the legacy this brought.

"We then explored the quintessential aspects of what makes a London event… and looking at something like Wimbledon we think that atmosphere of informality, laced with fun and festival, is really something we want to inject into London 2012," added Barrow.

"It does come down to the strawberries and cream and the long summer nights. We are trying to really create that type of atmosphere, albeit on a much bigger scale."

Lately, the golden torch is also issued that will be carried by the 8000 runners on the London 2012 relay.

The Olympic Flame will burn from a curved triangular aluminium tube which has a lace-like mesh complete with 8,000 holes—one to represent each torchbearer.

The triangular shape of the torch also symbolizes the three times that London has staged the Games—1908, 1948 and 2012. This is a special feat in Olympic history.

When the Olympics come to London in 2012, it will be the biggest party in town, and it's hoped the event will attract more visitors and businesses to the capital. But a new report suggests that that may not happen because previous Olympic cities have seen tourism stall rather than grow.

This could be one of the most spectacular settings in 2012. There's speculation about the Olympic rings going on Tower Bridge; a tourist's dream, you'd imagine. But not everybody believes that tourism will get a real boost from the games.

The European Tour Operators Association is clearly not convinced about the benefits of the Games.

Tom Jenkins (Executive Director) said, "I think the most important thing that people can do is look upon the Olympics as a great party, rather like a wedding. You have the party, enjoy that party, but don't think it's going to give you any lateral benefit. It won't."

Some say tourists will stay away because they fear hotel and restaurant prices will be too high, flights will be too packed and the capital will be overrun. Actually we found the opposite today.

Would you be put off coming to London during Olympics?

Visitor A: No, no I wouldn't. I would definitely go because London's an exciting city, and even with a lot of tourists around.

Visitor B: Well, if I want to come, I'll come. It wouldn't matter if there are more people; of course there would be more and of course it would be more expensive.

Despite this report the people responsible for selling London are still upbeat.

Martin Ainsworth-Wells (Marketing Director for Visit London): It's overtly pessimistic. Everything that we've learned from previous cities, everything that we know about London leads us to believe that the benefits are going to be big. We've already seen an increase in inquiries and bookings from event organizers, from conferences, from sporting event organizers, from now until 2012.

At the same time, the tickets sell like hot cakes, for example, more than one million ticket applications have been made for the men's 100 metres final at the London 2012 Olympics.

Only 40000 seats are available through the public ballot as the Olympic Stadium also has to accommodate sponsors, VIPs and the media—leaving the chances of securing a ticket extremely low.

The opening ceremony, for which £20.12 tickets were available to applicants, is also set to be oversubscribed by a considerable degree, meaning many could be left disappointed.

The 100 metres final was destined to be one of the most oversubscribed events but the sheer volume of applications—more than 25 times the available tickets—show the public's hunger for a slice of Olympic action has not been harmed by the lack of transparency in the process.

The London organizing committee says they have begun the process of taking money from ticket applicant's Visa accounts but they will not know until June 24 at the latest what events they have paid for.

One thing is certain. London can't just expect tourists to flock to the sites because of the Games. The capital will have to convince the world that there's something extra special about an "Olympic London".

## Notes

drizzly: 下毛毛雨的
congestion: 拥挤,堵车
quintessential: 精髓的,精粹的
transparency: 透明

# 伦敦奥运会堪比旅游经济？

上周，2012年伦敦奥运会的组织者公布了几幅艺术家的作品，这些作品描绘出几座尚未建成的临时奥运场馆在明年"全球最大盛会"伦敦奥运会举办时的模样。

观看伦敦奥运，不用介意伦敦潮湿且阴雨连绵的盛夏（温布尔登中央球场为此还安装了屋顶），也不用惦记机场式安检的严厉警示或交通拥堵。

伦敦奥运会的准备工作已步入新阶段，下月就将竖起"倒计时500天"的标牌。而这幅奥运"全景图"展示的场景是美味的草莓和奶油、公园野餐、街头派对以及漫长、慵懒的夏夜户外活动。

伦敦奥运建筑和场馆设计公司联合人众建筑事务所的一位高级负责人约翰·巴洛说："我们在两年前开始设计奥运场馆，主要着眼于节日气氛。"

"我们参考了1951年英国艺术节，还研究了战后改革时期人们的喜悦之情，我们也参照了这一时期留下的文化遗产。"

巴洛补充说："我们还探讨了在伦敦举办奥运盛会的闪光点，以及温布尔登等体育赛事元素。轻松、带有趣味性和节日风情的气氛是我们想在2012年伦敦奥运中展现的。"

"伦敦奥运将洋溢着草莓和奶油味道，以及英伦夏夜风情。我们将尽力在更大范围内营造这种气氛。"

伦敦近日也公布了2012年夏季奥运会的金色火炬，届时将有8000名火炬手接力传递。

2012年伦敦奥运圣火将在火炬内的三面锥体铝管内点燃，外层为花边网状结构,表面有 8000 个圆圈,代表 8000 名火炬手。

火炬的三面锥形设计还象征着伦敦举办的三届奥运会,分别在 1908 年、1948 年和 2012 年,表现了奥运历史上该城市的辉煌成就。

当奥林匹克运动会 2012 年在伦敦举办的时候,伦敦将上演一场最盛大的晚会,人们希望奥运盛会能把更多的游客和商机吸引到这个首都城市来。但最近一份报告显示,这种情形也许不会出现。因为从历届奥运主办城市的经历来看,游客人数非但没有上升,还有所下降。

这也许是 2012 年最盛大的场景之一,可以想象奥运五环来到伦敦桥塔,那是游客的梦想。然而,并非所有人都认为奥运能够实际刺激旅游业。

至少欧洲旅行社协会并不认为奥运会能使旅游业收益。

协会执行总监汤姆·詹金斯:"我认为人们能做的最重要的一点,就是把奥运会看作是一场盛大的晚会,而不是婚礼。你来到这场晚会,就尽情享受,但不要期望会有附带的获利,那是不会发生的事情。"

有人说,游客会因担心酒店和餐厅价格过高,机票太紧张以及城市太拥挤而刻意避开在这个时候前往伦敦。事实上今天我们听到了相反的声音。

你会因奥运而推迟你的伦敦之旅吗?

游客甲:不,我不会。我绝对还会去,因为伦敦是一个极其刺激的城市,即便人潮汹涌也如此。

游客乙:如果我想去,我还是会去,无论那里是否比平时有更多人。当然那时候人肯定多,消费也更贵。

尽管新出炉的报告对前景并不看好,但致力推销伦敦的人们依然乐观。

马丁·安斯沃斯—韦尔斯,伦敦旅游局营销总监,说道,有人过分悲观了。从历届主办城市的经验以及我们对伦敦的了解,我们有理由相信奥运给我们的回报会是丰厚的。来自活动组织方,各种会议和体育比赛组织方从现在到 2012 的咨询和预定数量都已经开始上升。

同时,伦敦奥运会比赛的门票也开始热销,例如,男子 100 米决赛的门票申请量已超过一百万。

# 美丽英文
## Beautiful English

因为奥林匹克体育场还需保证赞助商、贵宾及媒体的出席,以致公开发售的门票仅有四万张,使觅得一票的机会变得极为渺茫。

奥运会开幕式门票以20.12英镑的价格向申请者开放,超额订购现象亦相当突出,意味着许多人会失望而归。

100米决赛门票注定是超额订购最严重的赛事之一,然而超过可售门票25倍的申请量显示出公众对一场奥运赛事的渴望并未被缺乏透明度的购票过程所浇灭。

伦敦奥组委表示其已开始从门票申请者的维萨卡中扣费,但申请者最迟至6月24日才能知晓到底购买了何场赛事的门票。

有一点是毋庸置疑的,伦敦不能单凭奥运会让人们蜂拥而至。这座首都城市必须让世界相信,"奥运伦敦"还有其他方面的魅力。

## More to Read

英国伦敦旅游局高级代表、传播总监肯·凯林表示,伦敦旅游局期望从奥运旅游市场获利22亿英镑。而他也深知奥运旅游并不是一次性的投入与受益。凯林表示,伦敦奥运会对旅游业的影响将持续至2016年或2017年,在预期收入中,50%都是来自于奥运会后的长期受益,"很大一部分将来源于新兴市场"。在伦敦的这个目标市场中,很多人心目中的伦敦仍然还是"雾都"的景象,生活在其中的人们个个穿着古板的西装,手拿着雨伞走在雾气当中,"而实际上,我们现在是一个现代的、充满活力的大都市。"由此,在凯林看来,通过奥运会改变人们心目中伦敦的形象正是他们的一大目标。当天的展台设计也在努力改变人们对伦敦的看法,既有老牌旅游景点"大本钟",也有从千禧年才开始兴起的"伦敦眼",处处体现着传统与现代的融合。

观 察 OBSERVATION

## Reading Guidance

西尔维奥·贝卢斯科尼，现任意大利总理，意大利政治家和知名企业家，是意大利乃至整个欧洲的政经传奇人物。他衣着前卫，居然敢戴着头巾去迎接布莱尔；他为了再帅一点，不惜去整容挨刀子；他推出过情歌专辑，只为赢回老婆的心；他通过法律封杀八腿动物，只因他惧怕蜘蛛；他劝美国人来投资，出于对本国的漂亮 MM 有信心；他富可敌国，产业遍及意大利……一个很有"星味"的政治家，一个形象百变的"千面总理"。作为一个极具传奇色彩和争议的人物。好多人在质疑，这样的一个总理如何能够立足政坛？

# The Secret to Berlusconi's Dolce Vita

Real life in Italy is always one step ahead of anyone's imaginings. In the past few months, our political scene has started to resemble a spaghetti-western version of Mel Brooks's "Blazing Saddles"—anything goes. But we Italians are not laughing anymore. Some foreigners say: "It's all part of your charm!" At the center of the problem sits Silvio Berlusconi, who turns 75 this Thursday and is Italy's longest-serving postwar prime minister.

The whole world is well acquainted with Mr. Berlusconi's scandals and shenanigans—wild parties, prostitutes, unsavory business partners. Though he denies any wrongdoing, he is currently embroiled in no fewer than nine judicial tangles. The charges range from corrupting a witness to paying for sex with a minor.

This is embarrassing enough on its own, to say nothing of his government's pitiful record—stagnant GDP, rampant youth unemployment, stalled tax and justice reforms and fears over the public debt. But through it all—at least until recently—Mr. Berlusconi has been able to fall back on one abiding strength: He is the quintessential Italian and has been able to read the nation's mood like no one else.

Mr. Berlusconi represents some of the best, and much of the worst, of the national character. Every Italian possesses a tiny bit of Silvio. As the songwriter Giorgio Gaber summed it up:

*I'm not afraid of Berlusconi in himself*
*I'm afraid of Berlusconi in me.*

Here, then, are a few key terms to explain why Mr. Berlusconi has been around for so long—and why, despite being down, he's not yet out.

Simpatico. The most dangerous word in Italian is simpatico, means nice, likable, pleasant. But it can also mean putting on a seductive attitude, which is not always harmless.

What do many Italians think of Silvio Berlusconi? He looks like us. He's one of us.' He adores his kids, talks about his mamma, knows his soccer, makes money, loves new homes, hates rules, tells jokes, swears a bit, adores women, likes to party and is convivial to a fault.

He is our absolver in chief. He forgives us for the sins we have committed and those we may yet commit. "If they want upward of 50% of my income in

观察 OBSERVATION

taxes, I feel that's an unfair demand. I feel morally authorized to evade as much as I can," he said once.

"Am I faithful? Frequently," he quipped when confronted with the evidence of his serial adulteries. As details surfaced of his wild sex parties with girls who called him "Papi", he explained: "I work hard and, in the evening, I need to unwind."

Salesman. Mr. Berlusconi has brought to politics a flair for seduction that served him well in his previous careers in construction, television and advertising. He knows that his message has to be reassuring and easily digestible. And there are enough people in Italy who believe what they see in gossip magazines or on television—much of which Mr. Berlusconi owns or, as head of government, controls.

Mr. Berlusconi is convinced that, in a nation obsessed with appearances, image is key. In Italy, making the right impression too often prevails over doing the right thing.

Survivor. Every Italian feels he or she stands alone against the world, or at least the neighbors. Survival—personal, family, social and economic—is a source of pride and a test of ingenuity. Much has been written about Italians' individualism and resourcefulness, and Mr. Berlusconi embodies these qualities.

First he amassed his fortune, earning his spurs as a self-made man. Next, he built on Italians' distrust of everything shared, our intolerance of rules and the inner satisfaction that we take in finding private solutions to collective problems. In Italy, there is no real public pressure for a new, fairer tax system. People simply figure out ways to evade the one they already have.

Signore. Together with the Comune (municipality), the Signoria, or absolute lordship, is Italy's only indigenous political structure. All the others—feudalism, monarchy, totalitarianism, federalism, parliamentary democracy—have been imported from elsewhere. Their Italian incarnations have always been slightly artificial, from the toe-curling awkwardness of Mussolini's fascism to

today's passive parliament.

But a Signoria stirs ancient instincts, and many modern Italians see Mr. Berlusconi much as their forebears saw absolute lordships. We might satirize, circumvent or hoodwink the great prince, but we don't mess with him.

In Italy, the powerful do not have to exercise their power with restraint, as they do in other Western democracies. As the opposition called for his resignation, Mr. Berlusconi quipped, "They keep telling me, 'Go home! Go home!' They're putting me in a difficult position. I own 20 houses. Where shall I go?" Can you think of any other Western leader, in today's economic climate, who could get away with that?

Some things have not changed for centuries. The Signore's excesses are seen with a kind of bemused complicity, even pride. That is, until excesses become too excessive, as have Mr. Berlusconi's in the last few months.

Satanic Politics. Margaret Thatcher's classic acronym T. I. N. A. —There Is No Alternative—says it all about the attitude of Italian voters. The alternative to Mr. Berlusconi offered by Italy's center-left has proved unappetizing: strife-torn coalitions, woolly proposals, hypocritical posturing. And Mr. Berlusconi never fails to point out the communist roots of the rival Democratic Party.

Italians are realists. Before choosing what they think is right, they consider what they believe to be useful. In order to defeat the left, many Italians would have voted for the devil. Mr. Berlusconi can be pretty diabolical, but Satan's style is something else.

So, then, buon compleanno, Signor Silvio! Times are tough, and we have no present for you. Perhaps a farewell party instead?

## Notes

resemble：像，类似于

wrongdoing：坏事，不道德行为

观 察 OBSERVATION

embroil：使卷入纠纷
seductive：诱惑的
convivial：好交际的

# 贝卢斯科尼立足政坛的五种武器

意大利的真实生活总是让人始料未及。在过去的几个月里，意大利的政治图景就好像梅尔·布鲁克斯导演的西部片《灼热的马鞍》的意大利版本——任何事都有可能发生。但这一次，意大利人可笑不出来了。一些外国人说："这也是意大利风情的一部分！"问题的核心人物正是西尔维奥·贝卢斯科尼。上个月29日，他年满75岁了，成为意大利战后任职时间最长的总理。

对于贝卢斯科尼的丑闻和种种荒唐的举动——开狂野派对、召妓、结交声名狼藉的生意伙伴——全世界都已经耳熟能详了。尽管他否认自己做了任何错事，但他目前至少卷入了9件官司，面临着包括收买证人、与未成年人发生性交易在内等多项指控。

光是这些事就足以让人脸红了，更别提他领导下的意大利政府可怜的政绩了——国内生产总值停滞不前、年轻人失业率居高不下、税务和司法改革陷入困顿，还有公共债务引发的忧虑。但是，在经历了所有这一切之后，贝卢斯科尼一直——至少是直到最近为止——都能凭借一种持久的力量屹立不倒：他是典型的意大利人，比其他任何人都更了解国民的想法。

贝卢斯科尼的身上集合了意大利民族一些最棒的优点和大部分最烂的缺点。每个意大利人身上都有些许贝卢斯科尼的影子。正如流行歌曲作家乔治·盖博总结的那样：

> 我不怕贝卢斯科尼他本人，
> 我怕我自己意识里的贝卢斯科尼。

下面这几个关键词可以解释贝卢斯科尼为什么能这么多年稳坐总理宝座，以及他何以被打倒但却没有被赶下台。

第一个关键词是"讨人喜欢"。在意大利语中，最危险的就是这个词simpatico，它的意思是和蔼可亲、惹人喜爱、让人愉快。但这个词有时也用来形容某人摆出一副存心引诱人的态度，而这种态度并不总是无害的。

提起贝卢斯科尼，多数意大利人会想到什么？他看起来和我们差不多。他就是我们当中的一员。他很爱自己的孩子，经常谈起自己的妈妈，懂足球、会赚钱、喜欢新房子、讨厌清规戒律、爱开玩笑、有时会冒脏话、迷恋女人、喜欢开派对、纵情狂欢到了过分的地步。

他是我们的"首席赦免长"，他宽恕我们所有已经犯下的和可能会犯下的罪行。他曾经说过，如果他们想让我把50%以上的收入都用来交税，那我认为这种要求并不合理。从道德角度说，我觉得我有权尽可能多地逃税。

在面对一系列通奸证据时，他自我解嘲说，我忠诚吗？通常是的。当他和一群称呼他为"Papi"（意大利语中爸爸的意思）的女孩举行狂野性派对的丑闻细节被曝光后，他解释说，我工作很辛苦，到了晚上，我需要释放一下。

第二个关键词是"推销员"。贝卢斯科尼带着一种与生俱来的诱人魅力走进政坛，这种天赋帮助他在之前的建筑、电视和广告等职业生涯中取得了成功。他很清楚，他向公众传达的信息必须让人觉得安心而且浅显易懂。有足够多的意大利人会相信他们在八卦杂志或电视上得到的消息——许多此类杂志和电视台都归贝卢斯科尼所有，或者作为政府首脑，他能控制这些媒体。

贝卢斯科尼深信，在一个注重外表的国家，形象非常关键。在意大利，在公众面前留下好印象往往比做好事管用得多。

第三个关键词是"幸存者"。每个意大利人都觉得自己遗世独立,或者至少在邻居当中显得格格不入。无论对个人、家庭、社会还是经济角度来说,能够幸存下来都是件令人骄傲的事情,也是对机智的一种测验。有关意大利人的个人主义和权谋的作品琳琅满目,贝卢斯科尼就是这些品质的具体体现。

首先,他通过自己的努力积累财富,出人头地。其次,他进一步发扬了意大利人的特点:怀疑一切人所共知的观念、不能忍受清规戒律、在用个人方式解决集体的问题时内心会迸发出强烈的满足感。在意大利,公众不会真的向政府施压,要求实行新的、更公平的税收制度。人们只会去寻找逃避现有税收的方法。

第四个关键词是"贵族"。在意大利,土生土长的政治结构只有地方自治和贵族统治。其他所有的一切——封建制度、君主政体、极权主义、联邦制和议会民主制度——都是舶来品。从墨索里尼那令人难堪的法西斯主义到今天消极的议会,这些舶来品移植到意大利后总是有些不自然。

不过,贵族能够激发人们古老的本能。如今,许多现代意大利人看待贝卢斯科尼的方式就像他们的祖先看待专制贵族一般。我们可能会去挖苦、躲避或哄骗这位高高在上的亲王,但我们绝不会去干预他。

和其他西方民主国家不同的是,在意大利,掌权者在行使权力时不受约束。当反对派要求贝卢斯科尼辞职时,他用嘲讽的语气说:"他们不停地对我说'回家去!回家去!'他们真让我感到为难。我有20座房子,我该回哪个家?"在如今的经济环境下,你能想象其他任何一位西方领导人能不因这种言论受到谴责吗?

有些东西保持了几个世纪一直没有改变。贵族的暴行常被认为是一种不小心受到牵连的共犯行为,有时甚至还会引起他人的艳羡。前提是,暴行不要太过分,如果太过分了,比如贝卢斯科尼先生最近几个月内的所作所为,就会引发反弹。

第五个关键词是"魔王政治"。玛格丽特·撒切尔的经典缩略词"别无选择"极好地诠释了意大利选民的心态。意大利中左派提出的替代贝卢斯科尼的方案完全引不起选民的兴趣:冲突四起的政党联盟、含混不清的议案、伪善的姿态。而且贝卢斯科尼一直不遗余力地攻击竞争对手民主党的共产主义本质。

　　意大利人是现实主义者。在做出他们认为的正确选择之前,他们会考虑哪一个有用。为了击败左派,许多意大利人会投票给魔鬼。贝卢斯科尼有时可能比较穷凶极恶,但魔王风格是另外一回事。

　　那么,生日快乐吧,贝卢斯科尼先生!世道艰难,我们没有生日礼物可以送给你。或许,给你办一场欢送派对?

**More to Read**

　　在欧洲,贝卢斯科尼是个传奇而又极富争议的人物。无论是意大利大选前,还是贝卢斯科尼当选新总理的消息传出之后,欧洲主流媒体对贝卢斯科尼的批评铺天盖地,几乎掀起了一股"倒贝"潮。但以贝卢斯科尼为首的中右联盟在参众两院仍以绝对优势战胜了执政的中左联盟,贝氏领导的意大利力量党也以29.4%的得票率成为意第一大党,用欧洲主流媒体的话是"意大利向右转"了。工商巨子的利益与国家利益之间错综复杂的关系不能不让人们忧虑,大财团的支撑、没有强有力的反对派人选等因素使贝卢斯科尼避免了辞职下台的命运。然而,一个稳定的政府对意大利现在来说其实挺重要的,团结起来反而更有助于渡过目前的难关。

观 察 OBSERVATION

**Reading Guidance**

2008年的经济危机给美国人民带来的伤痛仍没有退去,近年来,油价持续飙升,失业率居高不下,财富过度集中,对中东、非洲等国家的军事行动,债务上限谈判陷入僵局……这些都大大影响了民众对国家的信心。诸多不利因素令奥巴马当初许下的"变革"承诺遭到质疑。如今,民众对奥巴马的很多说法并不买账,继而对整个政府都显示出不满,对民主党也表现出不信任。民调显示,多于七成的受访者认为经济问题是美国面临的最重要的问题,这一比例为2009年4月以来最高。在各类经济问题中,经济整体表现是受访者认为最重要的问题,其次是就业,联邦财政赤字问题排在第三位。甚至有较多美国人民认为美国迈入了错误的轨道。美国盖洛普公司近日日公布的民调显示,目前只有11%的美国人对国家现状感到满意,为2008年12月以来的最低水平。

# Nation's Mood at Lowest Level in Two Years, Poll Shows

Americans are more pessimistic about the nation's economic outlook and overall direction than they have been at any time since President Obama's first two months in office, when the country was still officially ensnared in the Great Recession, according to the latest *New York Times*/CBS News poll.

Amid rising gas prices, stubborn unemployment and a cacophonous debate in Washington over the federal government's ability to meet its future obligations, the poll presents stark evidence that the slow, if unsteady, gains in public confidence earlier this year that a recovery was under way are now all but gone.

Capturing what appears to be an abrupt change in attitude, the survey shows that the number of Americans who think the economy is getting worse has jumped 13 percentage points in just one month. Though there have been encouraging signs of renewed growth since last fall, many economists are having second thoughts, warning that the pace of expansion might not be fast enough to create significant numbers of new jobs.

The dour public mood is dragging down ratings for both parties in Congress and for President Obama, the poll found.

Disapproval of Mr. Obama's handling of the economy has never been broader—at 57 percent of Americans—a warning sign as he begins to set his sights on re-election in 2012. And a similar percentage disapprove of how Mr. Obama is handling the federal budget deficit, though more disapprove of the way Republicans in Congress are.

Still, for all the talk from Congressional Republicans and Mr. Obama of cutting the deficit as a way to improve the economy, only 29 percent of respondents said it would create more jobs. Twenty-seven percent said it would have no effect on the employment outlook, and 29 percent said it would cost jobs.

When it comes to cutting the deficit and the costs of the nation's costliest entitlement programs, the poll found conflicting and sometimes contradictory views, with hints of encouragement and peril for both parties.

Mr. Obama has considerable support for his proposal to end tax cuts for those households earning $250000 a year and more: 72 percent of respondents approved of doing so as a way to address the deficit.

And, in what he can take as a positive sign for his argument the nation has

观察 OBSERVATION

a duty to protect its most vulnerable citizens, about three-quarters of Americans polled think the federal government has a responsibility to provide health care for the elderly, and 56 percent believe it has a similar duty to the poor.

In what Republicans can take as a positive sign as they seek a more limited government, 55 percent of poll respondents said they would rather have fewer services from a smaller government than more services from a bigger one, as opposed to 33 percent who said the opposite, a continuation of a trend in CBS polls.

And slightly more Americans approve than disapprove of a proposal by Representative Paul D. Ryan of Wisconsin to change Medicare from a program that pays doctors and hospitals directly for treating older people to one in which the government helps such patients pay for private plans, though that support derived more from Republicans and independents. A recent Washington Post/ABC News poll that found 65 percent opposed Mr. Ryan's plan, suggesting results can vary based on how the question is asked.

Twice as many respondents said they would prefer cuts in spending on federal programs that benefit people like them as said they would favor a rise in taxes to pay for such programs.

Yet more than 6 in 10 of those surveyed said they believed Medicare was worth the costs. And when asked specifically about Medicare, respondents said they would rather see higher taxes than see a reduction in its available medical services if they had to choose between the two.

Given the choice of cutting military, Social Security or Medicare spending as a way to reduce the overall budget, 45 percent chose military cuts, compared with those to Social Security (17 percent) or Medicare (21 percent).

For the most part, Americans split sharply along party lines when it comes to whom they trust most on the deficit, Medicare and Social Security.

But with 70 percent of poll respondents saying that the country was heading in the wrong direction, the public was not exhibiting warm feelings toward officeholders of either party.

Most Americans think neither Mr. Obama nor the Congressional Republicans share their priorities for the country. Mr. Obama's job approval remains below a majority, with 46 percent saying they approve of his performance in office, while 45 percent do not. And support for his handling of the military campaign in Libya has fallen since last month: 39 percent approve and 45 percent disapprove.

Republicans have their own challenges. More than half of poll respondents, 56 percent, said they did not have a favorable view of the party, as opposed to 37 percent who said they did.

The nationwide telephone survey was conducted Friday through Wednesday with 1,224 adults and has a margin of sampling error of plus or minus three percentage points.

## Notes

ensnare：诱捕，使入圈套
cacophonous：不和谐的，粗腔野调的
dour：面无笑容的
respondent：调查参与者
a margin of error：误差

观察 OBSERVATION

# 美国人民不高兴

据《纽约时报》联合哥伦比亚广播公司新闻所做的调查结果显示,奥巴马总统开始执政的开始两个月,也就是美国正式陷入大萧条到现在,美国人对于国家的经济发展前景和整体趋势比以往任何时候都感到更悲观。

汽油价格不断上涨,失业成为顽疾,华盛顿不断有尖锐的言论攻讦联邦政府继续履行其未来义务的能力,在这种种乱象中这次的民调展示了一个明确的事实:即便今年早些时候虽然不算坚定,但公众信心还曾经有过缓慢的恢复,认为经济正在复苏,那么现在这点信心也消失殆尽了。

调查结果表明认为经济形势越来越差的美国人人数仅一个月就增加了13%,这一结果显示民意似乎是急转直下。即便自去年秋季以来出现了一些鼓舞人心的新的经济增长信号,然而许多经济学家在仔细思考后,警告说扩张的速率并不足以提供足够多新的工作机会。

民调发现,公众对政府的无好感态度使得对国会以及奥巴马的支持率正在下滑。

美国人对奥巴马执政时期的经济状况不支持率曾高达57%,这为奥巴马瞄准2012年的连任敲响了警钟。民众对奥巴马应对联邦预算赤字的反对率也达到了类似的百分比,对国会中的共和党反对率则更高一些。

对于国会中的共和党人以及奥巴马所决策的通过削减财政赤字来提升经济这一言论,也仅有29%的受访者认为会创造更多的就业机会。27%的人则表示这一举措对就业前景没有任何效果,另有29%的人还认为因此可能丧失工作机会。

当涉及削减财政赤字以及国家最昂贵的应得权益计划所需要的花销

时,民调显示出了相冲突甚至有时相矛盾的观点,而对于两党来说,既暗示着鼓舞又示意着危害。

结束对于年收入25万美元以上家庭的税务减免这一提议为奥巴马赢得了相当多的支持率:72%的受访者表示赞同通过这一手段来应对财政赤字。

一个国家有责任保护那些生活最困难的民众,奥巴马由此所实施的一些方案也为其政策带来了积极影响,大约四分之三的美国人投票认为联邦政府有责任为老年人提供医保,56%的美国人认为对穷人政府也应如此。

共和党人力求组建一个更加精炼的政府,在美国哥伦比亚广播公司所做的民调中,针对共和党人自认为积极有效的这一做法,55%的受访者表示,与其有一个庞大的政府来提供多种服务,倒不如从一个精简的政府中享有少量而优质的服务。但仍有33%的人持反对意见,并有增长的趋势。

来自威斯康星州的议员保罗·瑞安提出把医疗改革由原来把资金直接支付给医院和医生的模式转化为政府直接为这些病人支付私人医疗保险项目。对于这一提案,赞同者略多于反对者,但又从共和党人和独立选民那里得到了较多支持。

一些参与调查者表明,他们愿意通过提高缴税来支付政府实施的有利于民生的项目,而高于此两倍的受访者则声称,相比于此,他们宁愿联邦政府在这些项目上减少花销。

但多于六成的受访者相信医改是一项有价值回报的投入,当问及医改的具体方面,人们认为如果一定要在提高税收和减少有效医疗服务两者之间做出选择的话,大家宁愿选择前者。

当面临通过减少军队、社会安保、医疗改革的花销来削减统筹预算的选择时,45%的民众认为应削减军费开支,与17%的人选择社会安保,21%的人选择医改形成明显的对比。

大多数时候,当提及在财政赤字、医疗改革、社会安保方面更信任哪一个党时,美国人会按照政党阵营持有鲜明的不同观点。

但70%参与调查的美国民众认为整个国家正在迈入错误的方向,误入歧途。公众对任何政党的"朝中大臣"都没有显示出好感。

大多数美国人认为奥巴马和议会中的共和党人没能在对国家事务的决策上达成一致,意见不能共享。46%的民众对于总统先生执政期间的表现投支持票,同事也有45%的反对票,对其工作的认可程度仍低于半数。同时,对于其在利比亚的军事行动的支持率从上个月开始下降:39%的赞同票和45%的反对票。

共和党人自身也面临着挑战,56%——多于半数的受访者声明他们不看好共和党,仅有37%的人投了支持票。

全国范围内的电话调查已于本周三至下周五之间开展,共对1288名受访者进行了访问,抽样误差率为正负3个百分点。

**More to Read**

　　金融危机爆发3年来,尽管美国政府出台一系列应对措施,但美国经济却并没有走出衰退。今天的美国有着怎样的经济状况呢?最底层的人们感受最为直接:就业市场难以好转,社会保障体系入不敷出,收入差距不断扩大,整个国家层面的经济不景气。这样的民调结果可以说是当前美国社会矛盾的写照,它戳中了美国社会的痛处,是人们对日益扩大的贫富差距的不满以及对国家经济前途的担忧。后危机时代,大部分西方国家实体经济复苏迟滞,结构性失业难题短期无法解决,银行资产和家庭财富缩水,私人消费与企业投资萎靡,更有一些国家在财政赤字与债务的陷阱中难以自拔。对未来生活的沮丧和国家经济信心的缺失,正是当前西方世界所面临的共同社会心态。同时,也对国际变化所带来的影响:西方世界也许正酝酿着一场深层次的社会变革。

## Reading Guidance

　　发生在2001年9月11日的恐怖袭击给美国人无论从物质上还是精神上都造成了极大的影响。如今,"9·11事件"已经过去10年了,可时间并不能把此次恐怖袭击带来的伤痛减轻。10年了,美国人再次回到这个地方纪念遇难的同胞。人们的手指轻轻地划过纪念碑的大理石,寻找遇难家属的名字,想念他们在世时的样子。奥巴马也在"9·11事件"10周年的讲话中提到,灾难性的恐怖袭击给予了我们不断完善国家的机会,使我们有了新的价值观念,这些价值观念让我们的国家持续进步,让我们的民众团结一致。美国人民更加团结,历史是不能忘记的。

# The 10 Memorial Service of 911

　　Yesterday marked 10 years since the 9/11 attacks, when terrorists targeting the United States killed nearly 3000 people. New York, where the World Trade Center's North and South Towers collapsed in 2001. It happened after they were hit by two hijacked planes. It was where the biggest loss of life took place that day.

　　Commemorations were held at the sites of the attacks in New York, Washington and Pennsylvania. Ceremonies took place under extremely heavy security because of a credible but still unconfirmed threat of a possible new terror strike.

On Sunday, thousands gathered where the towers once stood, an area now known as Ground Zero. Those present paused for a moment of silence at 8:46 a.m., the exact time the first plane hit. It was the first of six moment of silence marking key moments of 9/11.

President Obama and former president George W. Bush, whom you saw right there, attended the ceremony, and they read passage from the *Bible*. Family member of those who died on 9/11 read aloud the names of each victim, and shared stores about their loved ones.

Peter Negron, son of 9/11 victim: "My father worked on the 88 floor of the World Trade Center. I was 13 when I stood here in 2003 and read a poem about how much I wanted to break down and cry. Since then, I've stopped crying, but I haven't stopped missing my dad. He was awesome. My brother, Austin, had just turned two when he passed. I've tried to teach him all the things my father taught me, how to catch a baseball, how to ride a bike and to work hard in school. My dad always said how important it was."

Observances were also held around the world to remember those lost, including hundreds from other countries. And in New York, a memorial opened as a permanent tribute to the events of 9/11.

The memorial took several years to plan, and it had many revisions along the way.

And nearby a tower even taller than the fallen towers is under construction.

Plans for a new and even taller skyscraper were revealed quickly, and changed repeatedly to make it stronger and safer. The new One World Trade Center will have a reinforced center core, extra fireproofing, biochemical filters and even green technology. Groundbreaking for the main tower, One World Trade Center, took place in 2006.

We are going to soar to new heights and reclaim New York's skyline with this magnificent symbol of our freedom.

Today, the still unfinished tower just pokes above the skyline on its way to becoming the country's tallest skyscraper, 1776 feet at the tip of its antenna, matching the year of U.S. independence, 1776.

In Washington, D.C., mourners gathered at the Pentagon, which also came under attack on 9/11.

Here, at 9:37 a.m., when in 2001, a plane struck the Pentagon, killing 184 people.

Vice President Joe Biden addressed those gathered, and spoke of America's resolve in the midst of a historic challenge. "Al Qaida and Bin Laden never imagined that the 3000 people who lost their lives that day would inspire 3 million to put on the uniform and harden the resolve of 300 million Americans. They never imagined the sleeping giant they were about to awaken. They never imagined these things, because they did not understand what enables us, what has always enabled us to withstand any test that comes our way. But you understood."

A third ceremony was held in a field in Shanksville, Pennsylvania. That's where another plane went down after passengers realized the hijackers' plans and tried to stop them from hitting a fourth target, thought to be the Capitol building in Washington.

Sunday, President Obama and the first lady laid a wreath in honor of the 40 passengers and crew members who lost their lives in that crash. It came a day after a new memorial was unveiled at the site.

The men and women aboard that flight will be remembered.

David Mattingly, CNN reporter: "Ten years ago, Shanksville, Pennsylvania, was the site of a violent act of terrorism. There was a great deal of uncertainty, fear and anger surrounding this site. Well, today, we find it completely transformed, this pastoral setting now very peaceful with grasses and wildflowers growing everywhere."

The dedication of this memorial today was for the bravery and courage of the passengers and crew of Flight 93, and it was an emotional time, not just for the family members of the people on board that plane, but also for former president George W. Bush. He says, "With their selfless act, the men and women who stormed the cockpit lived out the words, 'Greater love has no man than this, than a man lay down his life for his friends.'And with their brave decision, they launched the first counter offensive of the war on terror."

Right! We shouldn't just remember the people who died in the twin towers and those who died trying to save lives, but also the innocent people who died on the planes. Especially the brave people on the fourth plane—United Flight 93. It is important to remember 9/11 so that we can pray for all of the victims as well as their families that were involved in that horrible day. Even though 9/11 was an awful tragedy, it brought this country together and the unity shown after the attack should be an example of how to live our lives and how great our country is.

## Notes

hijack: 劫持, 绑架, 拦路抢劫
commemoration: 纪念
observance: 仪式
skyline: (以天空为背景的)轮廓线
resolve: 决心

# "9·11事件" 10周年纪念

　　昨天是"9·11恐怖袭击事件"10周年的日子。10年前的9月11日，恐怖分子袭击了美国，纽约世贸中心双子大厦遭袭击后倒塌，导致将近3000人丧生，造成了最严重的伤亡事件。

　　纪念仪式在纽约、华盛顿和宾夕法尼亚州当年遭到袭击的地方举行。由于有消息说恐怖袭击有可能会在9月11日当天发生，所以此次纪念仪式的安保规格相当高。

　　星期日早晨，数千人聚集在双子大厦曾经矗立的地方。现如今，这里被称作"归零地"。8点46分，聚集在这里进行悼念仪式的民众默哀，这正是当年恐怖袭击发生的时间。正是这6分钟的默哀拉开了"9·11事件"纪念仪式的序幕。

　　奥巴马总统和第一夫人米歇尔以及前任总统乔治·布什都参加了此次纪念仪式，他们宣读了《圣经》里的经文。"9·11事件"中的遇难者家属大声地喊着自己的亲人的名字，并且和别人分享着自己亲人的故事。

　　皮特·内格隆，一名"9·11事件"遇难者之子发言说："袭击事件发生时，我父亲正在世贸中心的88层上班。2003年的时候，我13岁。当我站在这里朗读一首诗的时候，我的眼泪夺眶而出。从那以后，我不再哭泣，然而我无法停止对我那令人尊敬的父亲的思念。我父亲去世的时候，我的弟弟奥斯汀才2岁。我一直在努力把我父亲教给我的东西教给我弟弟，比如如何打棒球，如何骑自行车以及要努力学习。我父亲经常提醒我这些是多么的重要。"

　　纪念仪式同时在世界上的其他地方举行，以纪念在"9·11事件"中遇难的外国人。在纽约,纪念仪式是对"9·11事件"永恒的敬意。

此次10周年的纪念仪式策划了好几年,中途经过多次修改。

在世贸中心的废墟上一座更高的摩天大楼正在建设当中。

修建一座更高的摩天大楼的计划很快就制定出来了,此项计划经过了数次修改,为的就是把摩天大楼建得更加稳固,更加安全。新建的世贸中心大楼会拥有更加坚固的核心,特殊的防火装置,生化过滤装置以及绿色科技。世贸中心大楼主楼的修建已于2006年破土动工。

我们将要打造新的高度,这一象征自由的高度会重新成为纽约的地标。

今天,正在建设中的新世贸大厦就要耸立在纽约市,它将成为美国最高的大楼,高达1776英尺(算上楼顶天线的高度),而1776恰好是美国独立的年份。

在华盛顿,哀悼的人群聚集在五角大楼,这里也曾是遭受"9·11"恐怖袭击的地方。

2001年,一架飞机袭击了五角大楼,造成184人死亡。

美国副总统乔治·拜登向参加纪念仪式的民众发表演说,他强调了美国在遇到历史挑战时的坚强决心:"基地组织和本·拉登绝对不会想到遇难的3000人会激励300万人团结起来,激起3亿美国人的决心。他们从未想到他们唤起了一个沉睡的巨人。他们从未想到这些,因为他们无法理解是什么激励着我们,让我们可以经受随时会遇到的考验。但是,你们都明白。"

另外一个纪念仪式在宾夕法尼亚州的尚克斯维尔镇举行。2001年9月11日,一架被恐怖分子劫持的飞机试图发动恐怖袭击,但被乘客制止,不幸的是飞机坠毁于此。这架飞机被据说是要袭击位于华盛顿的美国国会大厦。

星期天,奥巴马总统和第一夫人米歇尔为在恐怖袭击中遇难的40名乘客和机组人员献上了鲜花。就在前一天,一个新的纪念碑也在这里落成。

飞机上的人将会被人民所铭记。

美国有线电视新闻网记者大卫·马丁利说:"10年前,宾夕法尼亚州的尚克斯维尔镇是恐怖袭击的发生地。这里充满了不安,恐惧以及愤怒。然而,今天,我们发现这个地方已经彻底改变了。这里绿草如茵,鲜花遍地。"

此次纪念仪式是为了纪念93号航班上勇敢的乘客和机组人员。这是一个令人动情的时刻,不仅是为了遇难乘客的家人,还有上任美国总统乔治·布什。他说:"飞机上那些乘客用他们无私的行动,验证了一句话,那就是'相识莫过于此,为友可付生命'。他们用英勇的行为揭开了反击恐怖主义行动的序幕。

"是的!我们不应该仅仅记住那些在世贸中心双子大厦中遇难的人,那些奋力救人的人,我们还要记住那些无辜的遇难者,尤其是在93联合航班的人。铭记'9·11事件'对我们来说很重要,我们要为那些遇难者以及他们的家人祈祷。尽管'9·11事件'是一场悲剧,但是它使整个国家团结起来,这种团结告诉我们应该怎样生活,我们的国家有多么伟大。"

**More to Read**

2011年9月11号是美国"9·11事件"10周年纪念日,值此10周年之际,美国民众掀起了对"9·11事件"的纪念热潮,通过各种方式来纪念恐怖袭击事件中的遇难者。如今,恐怖袭击已经成为威胁人类的一大灾难。要解决恐怖主义问题,不能完全依靠某个国家的能力,也不能仅仅凭借暴力,而需要全世界热爱和平的人民团结起来共同解决!

观察 OBSERVATION

## Reading Guidance

> 随着新兴经济体的不断壮大，美国在全球经济份额中所占的比重在下降。中国作为世界上发展最快的新兴经济体，无论从贸易还是从金融上都有更多的话语权。随着中国在全球经济中的份额不断扩大，随之而来的便是汇率上的变化。随着贸易额的加大，以美元为结算工具的格局正在遭受着冲击。很多新兴的经济体都在和美元进行着较量，作为美国债权国的中国便是其中一员。作者从人民币和美元的竞争这一基点出发，认为中国最重要的是继续放宽金融市场。

# The Rise of the Redback

America's currency punches above its economy's diminished weight in the world. America's share of global output (20%), trade (only 11%) and even financial assets (about 30%) is shrinking, as emerging economies flourish. But many of those economies, such as South Korea, still sell their exports for dollars; many, including China, still peg their currencies to the greenback, however loosely; and about 60% of the world's foreign-exchange reserves remain in dollars.

  This allows America to borrow cheaply from the rest of the world. Its government has been able to overspend, secure in the knowledge that its IOUs will be bought by foreign central banks, which are not too fussy about price. America would show more self-discipline, many Chinese believe, if the dollar had a little bit more competition.

  Could the yuan become a rival? China's economy will probably surpass America's in outright size within 20 years. It is already a bigger exporter. It is prodding firms to settle trade and even acquire foreign companies in its own currency. That is adding to a pool of "redbacks" outside its borders. These offshore yuan are, in turn, being tapped by borrowers, issuing "dim sum" bonds in Hong Kong.

  But as the dollar's history shows, economic clout is not enough without financial sophistication. If foreigners are to store their wealth in yuan, they will need financial instruments that are safe, stable and easily sold. Dim sum makes for a tasty appetiser. But the main feast of China's financial assets is onshore and off-limits, thanks to its strict capital controls. The government remains deeply reluctant to let foreigners hold, buy and sell these assets, except under tight limits. Indeed, it is barely ready to give its own people financial freedom: interest on bank deposits is capped; shares are largely owned by state entities; and bonds are chiefly held by the banks—which are, in turn, mostly owned by the state.

  Over time China will relax its financial grip. But even if it could usurp the dollar's role as the world's currency, it will not replicate the American set-up. The United States takes advantage of the dollar's position to borrow cheaply from the rest of the world, selling its assets in return for goods. China is a mirror image of this. It runs a trade surplus, selling goods in return for financial claims on foreigners. Its firms, households and government save more than they can invest at home.

  No one will want to borrow in a currency that is only ever going to strengthen, increasing the value of their debts. So if China wants to "yuanify" some of its claims on the rest of the world, it will need a currency that can go down as well as up. To make people believe the yuan can fall tomorrow, China will have to loosen its currency's peg and let it rise faster today. China is different from America: it is a rising economic power and a thrifty one. But one rule still holds: China will have to open its financial system to the world if the yuan is to be the dominant currency.

## Notes

peg：使固定

clout：（政治上的）影响

sophistication：强词夺理，诡辩

# 美元，一家独大何时休

在全球范围内，美国所占的经济比重在降低，然而美元发挥的作用却与这一比重不相适应。随着新兴经济体的进一步发展，美国的出口额占全球总出口总额的20%，贸易额占全球总贸易额的11%，其金融资产也在进一步缩水（大约30%）。然而，这些新兴经济体中的很多国家，比如韩国仍在通过出口换取美元；也有很多国家，包括中国，仍在紧盯美元美元汇率，不过相对宽松；全球大约60%的外汇储备仍然用美元结算。

这使得美国能够以低廉的成本从其他国家借债。美国政府不知节俭，因为确信其他国家的银行会为其借据埋单，这些银行不会太纠结于美元价

格的变动。因此许多中国人认为，如果美元面临一些竞争，则美国能多表现出一些自律。

人民币会变成美元的竞争对手吗？在未来20年之内，中国的经济发展将会全面超过美国。中国的贸易出口额已经超过了美国。同时，中国也在鼓励外资企业在中国投资，甚至用以人民币为结算方式的办法来吸引外资企业。这增加了人民币在海外的竞争力。这些在海外投资的人民币反过来又被借贷者借出，用以在香港发行"点心债券"。

从美元的发展历史来看，没有金融因素的影响，经济因素对美元的影响是有限的。如果外国投资者想要以人民币为结算工具储蓄他们的财富，那么他们需要安全稳定以及易买卖的金融工具。"点心债券"恰好是一个不错的选择。然而，由于中国对金融资产的格控制，所以中国的金融资产投资主要限于国内投资，禁止国外资本投资。除了严格控制之外，中国政府一向不愿外国投资者持有、购买和出售这些资产。实际上，中国政府似乎没有做好给予国内投资者金融自由的准备：银行储备汇率有国家规定；国有企业持有大部分股票；国有银行持有大部分债券。

随着时间的推移，中国政府会慢慢放宽金融管制。然而，即使人民币取代美元成为了世界性货币，它也不会采用美国的货币组织方式。美国利用美元的地位从其他国家借贷货币，然后用这些货币购买物品。中国就是一个真实的写照。中国依靠贸易顺差成为了其他国家的债权人，然而中国国内的公司，家庭和政府部门的储蓄比在国内的投资要多。

没有人会愿意购买将会升值的货币，因为这意味着负债额将会增加。如果中国想要用人民币结算债务，那么它需要一种既可以贬值又可以升值的货币。为了让人们相信人民币能够贬值，中国必须改变盯住美元汇率的现状并且让人民币更快地升值。中国与美国不同：中国是一个新兴的经济增长体，而且讲求节约。然而，仍然存在一种规则：如果中国想让人民币成为统治性货币，中国必须向世界其他国家放开金融市场。

**More to Read**

众所周知,随着中国在世界经济中的份额不断加大,中国的话语权也在不断增强。随之而来的问题便是贸易的结算工具。当今世界,美元作为世界贸易结算的主要工具具有很大的作用。随着中国的世界贸易额不断地加大,改变以美元为结算工具的格局,进而以人民币为结算工具变成了一个迫切的需求。然而这又涉及人民币汇率的问题。中国政府在汇率这一问题上一向是很谨慎,美国一再要求人民币升值,而中国一直保持币值稳定。两国在这一问题上的分歧由来已久。因为人民币升值将导致中国的出口急剧下降,这对于中国来说是灾难性的。然而对于美国来说,则可以拉动就业。因此,人民币要想冲击美元的地位还需时日。

## Reading Guidance

现实生活中,大学之间的竞争很是激烈,大学排名能够帮助一些大学吸引更多的学生。本文作者认为大学之间也存在不平等,即使所谓的大学排名也会有不公正的现象。他认为大学之间应该在这种不平等的基础上进行合作,并引用《精神水平:为何更平等的社会总是做得更好?》一书来论证合作的重要性。学校排名不能够完全反映一个学校的真正水平,在评判一个大学水平的时候,要考虑很多因素。仅仅依靠排名就下定论是既不科学也不负责任的一种表现。

# Universities Should Work Together, Not Compete

Kate Pickett and Richard Wilkinson's "*The Spirit Level: Why More Equal Societies Almost Always Do Better*", published two years ago, hit neoliberal economics—and neo-conservative politics—where it hurt. For three decades after the election victory of Margaret Thatcher, the lucky and the privileged had consoled themselves that equality simply could not work—so they were off the hook.

Then Pickett and Wilkinson's book convincingly demonstrated, with graphs piled on charts piled on tables, not only that equality could work, but that it did work. More equal societies were not just fairer but more efficient—and everyone, rich as well as poor, did better.

But still the message has been resisted. Maybe there are two reasons for this. The first is that wealth generation, growth and efficiency were always a cover story. Instead of being a cruel necessity, the sad price that had to be paid, inequality is the end, not the means. Power, privilege, hierarchy—they are the whole point.

The second, perhaps more forgivable, reason may be that, post-Thatcher and post-Blair, acceptance of inequality has become a mindset from which it is difficult to escape. It has seeped into our collective view of the social fabric. Certainly something like this seems to have happened in higher education.

A new vocabulary has been invented—"top" universities, as opposed to the rest; "world-class" research, as opposed (presumably) to lousy research; and now "top" students, in other words those with AAB grades at A-level (who in fact often under-perform at university compared with their ungilded peers) gild.

Such language was hardly used in the past—although there has always been a pecking order of universities; successive research assessment exercises have identified research excellence for more than a quarter of a century; and universities have always used A-level grades as a self-congratulatory sieve.

Of course, it has its funny side. At least 25 universities confidently assert they are in the "top 10", and 25 more aspire to be there in the very near future. Methodologies that would be rejected in an undergraduate essay are uncritically accepted in league tables, provided they produce the "right" result.

But, returning to *The Spirit Level*, this enthusiasm for inequality has its darker side. First, inequality featherbeds the fortunate. So we are expected to believe that Newcastle is better than Durham or Liverpool than York, Similarly, supposing that historically determined hierarchies are orders of contemporary merit is silly. Of course, Cambridge is "better" than London Metropolitan; it has had seven centuries' start.

Second, and more seriously, enthusiasm for inequality undermines the solidarity of higher education which, following Pickett and Wilkinson, is a source of strength not weakness. Most obviously, it allows politicians (and Treasury cost cutters) to divide and rule. It is truly remarkable—and shameful—that the armed services, despite being divided into three warring branches, work together better than universities, which have much less to separate them in the competition for resources.

But, more fundamentally, the efficiency, success and strength of higher education depend on habits of solidarity. The standard of degrees is maintained by a cat's cradle of external examiners. The quality of research applications, and of books and other publications, relies on academic referees. Lectures and seminars also depend on this culture of academic altruism.

There is already alarming evidence of the breakdown of these habits of solidarity. Altruism no longer applies outside narrowing "tribes" of universities.

## Notes

hierarchy：等级制度
fabric：构造，组织
altruism：利他主义

## 大学需要合作，而非竞争

凯特·皮科特和理查德·威尔金森的《精神水平：为何更平等的社会

## 观察 OBSERVATION

总是做得更好?》一书出版于两年前,这本书抨击了新自由主义经济模式以及新保守主义政治模式。自玛格丽特·撒切尔大选获胜以来的30年中,那些幸运的享有特权的阶层不断自我安慰,平等无法让人工作,因此他们为自己开脱了。

皮科特和威尔金森的这本书以图文结合的方式证明了平等真的可以促进工作,很有说服力。平等水平高的社会不仅更加公平而且效率更高——人们无论贫富都做得很好。

然而,书里的观点还是不被认可。或许有如下两个原因。第一,财富增长和效率通常只是一种托词。人们不是必要,而是必须支付令人难以接受的价格,不平等是目的而不是手段。政权、特权、等级就是全部。

第二个原因或许可以为人理解,那就是在后撒切尔和后布莱尔时代,人们对不平等的接受已经成为一种精神状态,这种精神状态是难以摆脱的,它已经成了整个社会的共识。类似的情况似乎已经在高等教育领域中发生过。

人们创造出"'顶尖'大学"这个词以和其他学校相区分;人们创造出"'世界级'研究"这个词,以和其他低水平(假定是这样)的研究相区分;人们创造出"'尖子'生"这个词,另外还有AB级水平的说法(实际上,这些"尖子生"在大学里的表现与他们的称号很不相符)。

这样的词语在过去几乎是不用的——即使大学里也存在着等级之分;用评估的方式来确定研究的优劣,已经持续了25年,有些大学使用A级来自欺欺人。

当然,也有滑稽的一面。至少有25所大学很自信地宣称自己排名前十,其他的大学也渴望着自己能够在不久的将来进入前十的行列。假如大学排行榜给出了"正确的"排名,那么它就等于是不加鉴别地采用了连研究生论文都拒绝使用的方法。

然而,当我们返回去参看《精神水平》一书时,会发现对于热衷于不平等也有不好的一面。首先,不平等会使一些人担任闲职。因此,我们有望相信纽卡斯尔大学比杜尔汉姆大学要好。相似的情况还有,依据学校办学历史来对大学排名也是一件很愚蠢的事情。当然,剑桥大学比伦敦城市大学要"好",就在于剑桥大学已经有超过700年的历史了。

其次,更为糟糕的是,热衷于不平等会影响高等教育机构之间的协作。根据皮科特和威尔金森的理论,高等教育之间的协作可以提高协作双方的实力,而不是减弱。更为明显的是,它允许政客(以及主张减少政府财政支出的人)在学校里管理担任职务。值得注意但同时也让我们感到不快的是——海陆空三军,尽管被分为三个兵种,但是他们之间的通力合作也比大学之间的合作要强,更不用说把大学分等以此来竞争教育资源了。

然而,从深层次上讲,高等教育的效率、成功和实力依靠的正是合作。但是,这些结果却让一些校外评估人员把持着。研究应用、书籍以及其他出版物的质量都由一些学术鉴定专家来评定。学术报告和研讨会也依赖于学术利他主义。

令人担忧的是,高等教育合作破裂的迹象已经很明显地显现出来了。除了限制大学之间的分裂现状,利他主义已经没什么用武之地了。

**More to Read**

似乎我们每个人都很关注每年一些机构推出的大学排名,无论世界范围内的,还是国内的。这些排名在某种程度上左右了人们对大学的看法以及评价,进而影响了莘莘学子的择校,以至于很多学校都宣称自己是排名靠前的学校。更深层次的则是大学之间的无休止的竞争,这种竞争表面看上去是公平合理的,实则有很大的隐患,无论对大学自身发展还是对学生择校都产生了很大的影响,甚至可以说这种影响很大程度上是负面的。另外,大学进行排名的机构和操作机制合理吗?这同样是值得我们怀疑的地方。不能排除,为大学排名的机构会通过一些不正常的手段偏袒某些大学。基于这样的认识,我们要慎重对待大学排名,不要人云亦云。不要被某些表象的东西所蒙蔽,要看到事情的本质,这样才能抓住核心。

观察 OBSERVATION

Reading Guidance

　　11月11日是美国"老兵节",这一节日起源于第一次世界大战。战后,交战双方商定,休战日被视为世界大战实际结束的那天。1919年,美国总统威尔逊宣布11月11日为"休战日"(Armistice Day)。1938年,美国通过法律,将休战日设为法定假日。后来美国又经历了第二次世界大战,有更多人参加了战争。于是,在老兵组织的推动下,1954年正式改名为"老兵节",以纪念历次战争中牺牲的将士,为幸存的老战士祝福。"老兵节"的日期曾经有过一次变动。1968年通过法律,规定每年11月的第二个星期一为"老兵节",这样人们就可以享受三天假期了。但美国很多州都不同意改变日期,认为11月11日具有特殊的历史意义和爱国主义价值,不得已,联邦政府在1975年又改回原来的日子。这一天是公共假日,学校和政府部门都要放假。近几年,美国人把"老兵节"渐渐变成祈祷和平的节日,在这一天,人们把一束束鲜花和花圈敬献在英魂墓碑前并向死去的战友致意,总统也会出席在弗吉尼亚州阿灵顿国家公墓等地所举行的纪念活动。

# Veterans Day for No More War

　　The United States observes Veterans Day November 11, a national holiday to remember and honor military veterans of all wars. Veterans Day dates back to

〈193〉

the end of World War I in 1918.

Inside a classroom at Santa Monica College, a group of students meet once a week to make friends and for support. They are all military veterans, and for some, the horrors of war are still very real.

"When I came home it took three years to transition after getting out. That was such a feeling of being lost, that we were given no transitional training, no decompression," Monica Scates said.

Scates served in the first Gulf War against Iraq 20 years ago. When she returned home she was suffering from post-traumatic stress disorder.

"I lost my marriage. I lost my family, my home," she said.

Scates eventually received treatment, and has just started college.

Fellow Army veteran Daniel Anderson served in both Iraq and Afghanistan. He joined the military shortly after finishing high school. "I gave myself an ultimatum. If I don't do well in college, I'll join the military," Anderson said.

Another veteran of the war in Afghanistan, Christopher Bellingham, joined the Army for the education benefits that military service provides.

"I wanted some money for college," Bellingham said.

While these three Army veterans had military experience under combat conditions, their views about America's future course in Iraq and Afghanistan are not the same.

Scates says U.S. troops should not leave Iraq at the end of this year. "To be honest with you, no, because it will be just like what we did during Vietnam. We have to stabilize the people first. They don't have a stable government. They don't have a stable force," she said.

Anderson disagrees. "I think it's about time that we pull out because they, I think, are ready to stand up take it on their own," he said.

Anderson says he is not sure whether the fight in Iraq was worth the cost, in either human or military terms.

"I'm glad Saddam Hussein was ousted from power. And there is a lot of corruption, and you can see it. But that's just a much more muddied water, you know. I think that war was a political, strategic war, as opposed to a necessary, on-the-ground fight," Anderson said.

Bellingham says the U.S. should also get out of Afghanistan.

"There's no purpose any more. We've pumped so much money in that economy that we are their GDP (their entire economy). We are how they're making money now. Regardless of when we pull out, they're not going to be able to sustain to the level we brought them up to. The longer we're there, the more damage we bring." Bellingham said.

But Anderson says the Afghan people need U.S. help against the Taliban.

"I think the people are really oppressed by that terrible organization. I think that one is really worth fighting for," he said.

All three veterans say they don't think the Americans fully understand what their troops are fighting for in Iraq and Afghanistan. In part, they blame the American news media.

"The 'talking heads' on TV. It gets lost in opinion as opposed to fact," Anderson said.

For these veterans, their experiences in the military are shaping their future plans.

Monica Scates wants to help homeless veterans.

"I want to work with troubled vets, I want to get them off the streets," Scates said.

Christopher Bellingham wants to conduct research on brain disorders, such as post traumatic stress syndrome.

"Definitely experiencing and seeing my friends go through PTSD, and their emotional coping, piqued a greater curiosity and drive," Bellingham said.

Anderson wants to be a screenwriter, to tell the story of what he saw.

Their experiences in war changed the lives of these three veterans, and

they hope that life experience will enable them to change the lives of others—the people they will touch in their future careers.

## Notes

veteran：老兵，退伍军人
transition：过渡，变迁
decompression：减压，解压
ultimatum：最后通牒
screenwriter：剧作家，编剧

# 为和平而生的"老兵节"

11月11日是美国的"老兵节"。在美国，这是一个全国性的假日，纪念所有参与过各项战事的军人。"老兵节"可以追溯到1918年第一次世界大战结束的日期。今年的"老兵节"，距离美国从伊拉克撤军不到两个月的时间，但是美国依然有将近10万官兵驻扎在阿富汗。

圣莫尼卡大学有几个学生每个星期都要到的一个教室聚会，交友，同时也是为了彼此之间相互支持。他们都是在军队里服过役的。对于其中一些人来说，战争的恐怖至今还历历在目。

莫尼卡·斯盖茨说："我退役回家之后，整整花了3年的时间，调整心态。那时候感到不知所措，而且也没有接受任何调整心态、回到正常生活当中的培训。"

20多年前斯盖茨在第一次海湾战争中服过役。她从战场上退下来以

观察 OBSERVATION

后,明显感受到了自己患有创伤后精神紊乱症。

她说:"我的婚姻破裂,家人离我而去,住房也没了。"

后来,斯盖茨得到了治疗,她开始到社区大学念书。

丹尼尔·安德森也是一位退役军人。他在伊拉克和阿富汗都服过役。安德森是高中毕业后不久参军的。他说:"我给自己下了一条命令,要是书念得不好的话,干脆就入伍参军。"

谈到为什么要入伍参军,克里斯托夫·贝林汗姆则说,他之所以入伍是因为看中了参军以后,军人能够享受的那些教育方面的福利。贝林汗姆在阿富汗战事中服役。

虽然上面提到的这三位退役军人都亲历过战事,但是他们对美国在伊拉克和阿富汗战事的前景,却有着不同的看法。

斯盖茨说,美国不应该在今年年底之前,从伊拉克全部撤军。她说:"我的想法是,不应该;因为如果撤军的话,结果就跟我们在越战中的做法没有什么不同。我们应该先把当地的局势搞定,那里目前没有一个稳定的政府,也没有一个稳定的军队可言。"

但是,安德森则不这么想。他说:"我认为,应该撤军了,因为我看他们已经准备好,能撑住的。"

安德森说,美国对伊拉克的战事,无论是从军事的角度、还是从人的付出的角度来说,都很难说是不是值得。

他说:"我很高兴萨达姆·侯赛因被赶下台了,现在腐败很严重,是看得到的。不过,那场战事本来就不是那么明朗,在我看来,那是一场政治性的、战略性的战事,而不是完全有必要展开的、必须打的战争。"

贝林汗姆认为,美国不仅应该从伊拉克撤军,也应该从阿富汗撤军。

他说:"现在已经没有什么目标可言了,我们在那儿投入了这么多的钱,我们实际上就是他们的国民生产总值,就是他们赚钱的方式。不管什么时候撤军,他们都没有能力保持我们帮助他们达到的那个水平。留守的时间越长,后患越多。"

不过,安德森说,阿富汗人需要美国的帮助,来对付塔利班。

"我认为,当地人确实是受到塔利班这个坏透了的组织的压制,我认

〈197〉

为,阿富汗战事还是很值得打的。"

三位退役军人都说,普通的美国人根本不能充分理解美国出兵到伊拉克和阿富汗是为了什么。他们说,这在一定程度上,是媒体造成的。

安德森说:"电视上那些专搞评论的,他们只是侃侃而谈,根本没有着重事实。"

对这些退役军人来说,军旅生涯对他们的一生都有着不可磨灭的影响。

斯盖茨说她要帮助那些无家可归的退役军人。

"我想要帮助那些有障碍的退役军人,不让他们无家可归。"

贝林汗姆打算在大脑功能失调方面进行研究,比如说,研究创伤后精神紊乱症。

他说:"不用说,看到我那些朋友们经历创伤后精神紊乱症,如何艰难地挣扎,这对于我来说,都是动力。"

与此同时,安德森说,他想要当一名剧作家,把自己的所见所闻,告诉世人。

亲历战事,无疑改变了这三名退役军人的人生。他们都希望能够借助自己的人生经历,通过未来的职业生涯,让他人生活得更美好。

## More to Read

美国的"老兵节"是纪念为国牺牲和奉献的美国老兵的日子。在历次战争中,除了美国的国内战争,第二次世界大战是美国蒙受了最大伤亡的战争,美军一共阵亡40万人。军队是国家的基石与根本,而军队又是由个体的"人"组成的。美国的节日为什么不纪念"军队"而只纪念"军人"呢?也许他们更在乎这些为了国家利益而不惜抛头颅洒热血的将士,因为他们是父母的儿女,儿女的父母,妻子的丈夫,丈夫的妻子,更重要的是他们是军人,一些能为了素不相识的人的安危和幸福去牺牲自己生命的勇士!近年来,美国不停地向海外出兵,例如攻打伊拉克、阿富汗等地,造成美军伤亡人数达到历史最高值,这样的战争对于参战的士兵及其家人是永远不可磨灭的伤痛。唯有抵制霸权主义和侵略战争,才能让世界人民真正享有安宁与和平。